Young Vines

James Russell
Lingerfelt

W&K
William and Keats Publishing™

Published by WilliamandKeats.

WILLIAMANDKEATS is a registered trademark of WilliamandKeats Publishing.
Copyright © 2019 by James Russell Lingerfelt. All rights reserved.
Cover Photo by Ben Goode. Development editing by Donna Cook. Line editing by Elisabeth McKetta.

Library of Congress Cataloging-in-Publication Data
Lingerfelt, James Russell. Young Vines
ISBN-13: 978-0-9844766-9-5
ISBN-10: 0-9844766-9-5

ISBN-13: 978-0-9844766-9-5
ISBN-10: 0-9844766-9-5

Printed in the United States of America

Table of Contents

Chapter 1	1
Chapter 2	5
Chapter 3	11
Chapter 4	17
Chapter 5	23
Chapter 6	35
Chapter 7	45
Chapter 8	51
Chapter 9	63
Chapter 10	71
Chapter 11	83
Chapter 12	89
Chapter 13	95
Chapter 14	101
Chapter 15	111
Chapter 16	117
Chapter 17	125
Chapter 18	135
Chapter 19	143

"In times of pain, when the future is too terrifying to contemplate and the past too painful to remember, I have learned to pay attention to right now. The precise moment I was in was always the only safe place for me. Each moment, taken alone, was always bearable. In the exact now, we are all, always, all right. Yesterday the marriage may have ended. Tomorrow the cat may die. The phone call from the lover, for all my waiting, may not ever come, but just at the moment, just now, that's all right. I'm breathing in and out. Realizing this, I began to notice that each moment was not without its beauty." – Julia Cameron, *The Artist's Way*

Young Vines

Chapter 1

I remember the first time I ever thought about my wife. I was seven years old, my parents were still alive and loved each other, and it was Christmas. We lived in a brick home in the foothills of the snowcapped mountains of Calgary, Alberta.

Though the fogged sun had already set, my parents hadn't turned on the end table lamps in our living room. The walls glowed from the twilight outside, and on our tree hung Christmas lights of green, crimson, and icy blue. Mom was lying in Dad's arms in the silence, as he ran his fingers through her hair. I remember watching them and wondering where my wife was.

During my freshman year of college, I was single, but my wife–whoever she would be–had always been in my thoughts since that Christmas. I wrote letters to her in middle and high school, which I kept in a journal, and I gave them to my wife Joanna on our wedding night. She read them as she sat on our hotel bed in the hills above Lake Como, Italy, and cried. Those letters meant the world to her.

If you had told me how all of our dreams would have ended, I wouldn't have believed it. I wouldn't want to. For I was led to believe that if I was a good person, then I would live a good life with a happy wife, and my life and wife would be good and happy forever.

I'm almost forty years old now and things haven't turned out at all the way I had imagined. But I'm okay with that because I'm happy, despite all that happened.

My name is Ryan Lockwood, and this is a simple love story from my life about a boy who loved a girl.

⸎

It was 2009, spring in Southern California. Ten years had transpired since my friends and I graduated from Pepperdine University in Malibu. This was the year the movie Avatar debuted and Miley Cyrus was breaking from her Disney shell. That year, a US Airways plane landed in the Hudson River and they made a movie about it years later, starring Tom Hanks. In that same year, four Somalian pirates seized *The Maersk Alabama*, holding its crew captive, and a movie was made about that years later too… starring Tom Hanks.

Barack Obama became the first African-American United States president and won the Nobel Peace Prize.

A lot can happen in a year.

A lot happened in my year.

I was a literature professor at my alma mater, teaching an occasional course on society and culture. My dream since graduate school was to become the Chair of the program that developed my career. I had attended the University of Calgary as an undergrad and started grad school at Pepperdine when I was twenty-three. I had wanted to be a professor ever since I was a kid, and I knew I could achieve it if I worked and studied hard enough. As one of my mentors said, "It isn't the smartest people who have PhDs, but the most persistent." To be Chair, you had to be voted for by the other professors and approved by the Dean of the university, so reputation was everything.

Knowing I could spend the rest of my life at Pepperdine brought me a lot of comfort. Most of the buildings face the ocean and have glass walls so everyone can enjoy the beautiful views. All the buildings are painted coral and have clay shingled roofs. The campus sits on a hill overlooking the Pacific Coast: an electric-blue ocean with tangerine sunsets behind cedar-green mountains.

Mist falls from the tops of the Santa Monica mountains, and the scent of salt rolls in from the Pacific Ocean. At night, from the ocean, Malibu looks like a necklace of lights along the coast, less gaudy than the brighter-lit cities nearby: Santa Monica, West Hollywood, and Beverly Hills. Malibu only had 12,000 people living in the city limits back then, and I preferred small towns. The mayor shut everything down at 10 p.m., even the bars, to keep out trouble. Locals found entertainment away from the movies by building fires on their private beaches, making the town feel more like a retirement community.

Pepperdine is where I met my best friends and my wife Joanna. It's where I fell in love for the first time, and it holds some of the greatest memories of my life. That, and the summers I spent at my grandmother's vineyard in Tennessee.

My grandmother used to say that if you have just one true friend you're wealthy. Only at Pepperdine did I really understand this to be true.

It was a Friday when I was leaving my office. I had received a letter from a lawyer's office in Nashville, delivered to the literature department. Finals week had just ended, which meant I could rest, so there was no rush to read the letter. I didn't know anyone in Nashville, so as far as I was concerned, it was junk mail. I dropped it on the passenger seat of my car, and carried on.

Chapter 2

I had been invited to dinner by Dr. Willis, the Chair of the Literature Department. He had been my professor in graduate school and now he was my colleague. I liked and respected him a lot. We were to meet at 6 p.m. at Marmalade Café, a trendy spot built to look like a café you'd find in Rome. Beige and brown brick had been made to resemble stone, with Roman archways and murals of second-century Roman life painted on the walls.

I had been teaching all day, so I was mentally drained. I shaved and showered. I gave myself a good look in the mirror after I slid into my trusty black suit and crisp white dress shirt. I had bought the suit in Romania in 2001 while spending a summer teaching English. It was very well made, with four buttons, and had cost one third of the price I would have paid in the States.

Traffic is never bad in Malibu, especially on the back roads to downtown. I drove a used silver Toyota Camry, which I had paid off, and I parked beside the

Malibu Market, a grocery store that baked its own goods and sold fresh fish caught that morning. I've seen a few Hollywood movie stars there. Jason Statham wears hats, Brittany Spears wears hats, Pamela Anderson wears sunglasses, Jerry Seinfeld wears hats and sunglasses, but Ted Danson and John Cusack wear neither and will chat it up with anyone.

When I entered the restaurant, I could feel the warmth of the ovens and could smell the fresh baked lasagna. A college student with her hair pinned up led me through the crowded room lit by bronze ceiling lights. The staff wore pressed black dress shirts and slacks.

Dr. Willis was sitting at a table and talking on his cell phone. He motioned me over when he saw me. He had a full head of salt and pepper hair and wore a blue pinstriped suit, with a yellow tie. His glasses sat on the tip of his nose, and for a man in his sixties, he looked ten years younger. No one had taught in the literature department longer than Dr. Willis, and he had served as the Chair for fifteen years.

He stood to shake my hand, and made some last comments on the phone, for which he apologized after he hung up. After he asked me about traffic, the waitress took our orders. Mine was steak and his was salmon.

"How're classes going?" he asked me. Classes were over, but I knew what he meant. For the next thirty minutes we chit-chatted through dinner about grading papers, underperforming students, and complaining parents. He asked me how I was dealing with losing Joanna. Two years had passed since then, and I appreciated him still asking. It didn't seem like two years. It felt more like six months. I gave Dr. Willis a short and satisfying answer and I didn't dive deeper than that. I had learned that people don't want to hear a lot about your sadness and loss.

Besides, I could tell that something was on his mind. We had sat at the same table at many events, and I had even shared some meals with him and his wife throughout the years, but he had never invited me to a night out, just us, before.

"So, I have some news for you," he said, cheerfully. "It's not final yet, but I'm retiring."

"Congratulations," I answered, breaking out into a huge grin, because I knew where the conversation was going.

"Chair will be open. I know how much it means to you." His smile widened, and the candlelight reflected off his glasses. I lifted my wine and offered a toast. He raised his and we clinked them together.

"Are you staying here?"

"I think so," he responded, tentatively. "I might do some adjunct work."

I nodded, happy for him. "So, what do I do?"

"Well, I talked to Dean Davis and said good things about you. I don't think you'll have a problem winning over the other faculty. They all like you and know what you're about."

This was good news for all the reasons I could imagine. Not only did I have a shot at being the Chair, but Dr. Willis wasn't moving to another town. He would teach part-time when our department needed him. And with the student debt I still had, an increase in pay for Chair would help a lot. It was strange, but in that moment I thought of my grandmother, who spent her life tending a vineyard in Tennessee. I could almost hear her saying, "Persistence and consistency. Slow and steady wins the race."

When I left Marmalade's I felt lighter. So much of what I had striven for since I was a college student was now within reach. Chair was almost a certainty.

I walked back into my condo. The living room sat on the left with a TV, couch, and recliner I rarely used. The kitchen was straight ahead and the back wall was a giant window with a door and patio that overlooked campus and the coast. The windows stayed open during the day to keep the air fresh, but I closed them after dark because, for some reason, the night air always gave me a cold.

I emptied my pockets onto the kitchen counter. My car keys and cell phone. Other than a few clothes and pairs of shoes lying around my bedroom, I kept the rest of my condo clean and tidy, despite the reputation of how single men live.

After Joanna passed away, I didn't give the condo any additional personal touches. I left her clothes in our closet. The only thing I changed was to hide a vase she loved in the back of the cabinet below the sink.

I opened the refrigerator to check if I needed groceries. Nope. I had the basics I always kept around. Milk, orange juice, eggs, avocado, bacon. A bottle of juice I made from kale, celery, carrot, cucumber, apple, ginger, lemon, and lime. My friend Oz had put me onto juicing back in college, but Joanna never took to it. She said the green stuff made her gag. I checked the pantry. Bread and peanut butter and a can of assorted nuts.

At home, I sometimes treated myself to an occasional glass of wine or an Old Fashioned. Sometimes, I paired it with one of the Cuban cigars I brought back from Calgary. Other than that, I took care of myself health-wise, better than average at least. And I worked out at Pepperdine's gym four days a week.

My counselor, Dr. Cates, had told me to watch my health during the years I mourned Joanna. He had seen men eat and drink themselves to death. Eating right and exercising would help with the endorphins and fight depression too. And I knew Joanna would want me to do well in life. Dr. Cates believed it, too. He said that Joanna wouldn't want me to forever mourn my loss of her and our future children, but that she would want me to move on and find happiness again.

I poured a glass of Pinot Noir and changed into my Pepperdine basketball shorts and a t-shirt. I plopped onto the couch and saw C.S. Lewis's *A Grief Observed* sitting on the end table.

My college friend Finn had mailed it to me. Lewis wrote it after his wife had passed away. I had read many of Lewis's books, but not that one. I didn't feel like reading it, so I pulled my laptop out instead. I wasted some time on Facebook until my eyes were so heavy that I knew I'd pass out as soon as I went to bed. And that was good because on most nights I lay in bed missing Joanna.

Chapter 3

The next morning, I woke up glad that I had shut the blinds on my windows. I didn't like the sunshine so early in the morning. I had loved the morning light when Joanna was alive. We'd wake at dawn, and make love, and we'd drink coffee at the table as the sun rose. The morning sun now only reminded me that such times with her would never happen again. Plus, I knew I needed my sleep.

Dr. Cates had explained to me that lack of sleep sends people into clinical depression faster than anything else in the world. "And believe me," he had said, "That's not a state you want to be in." The chemicals in the brain lock into a new equilibrium and the only way out of clinical depression is medication, and, if it gets extreme, it can end in suicide or a mental hospital.

The buzzing from my cell phone roused me, and I remembered that Oz and I were supposed to grab brunch at Coogie's in Malibu. It's called Ollo now, more chic and modern, but we still call it Coogie's. Back then it was a bright, energetic café that served everything from pancakes to gourmet steak.

I cracked my eyes and looked at the phone.

"Hey man," I said to Oz, not hiding the early morning struggle in my voice.

"Just wanted to make sure we're still on. I didn't want you oversleeping. I sent you a text. Did you get it?"

"Not yet."

"You okay?" he asked.

"Yeah. Yesterday was a good day actually."

"Cool," he said. "You can tell me about it at brunch. I have some good news."

"What?" I replied.

"That study abroad program in Kenya was approved, so your boy is going to Africa for a few weeks."

"Congrats, man," I told him. Oz had been working on that for over two years. He launched the study abroad program in Ireland a few years before and the students loved it.

"Thanks," he said. "We'll celebrate. I'll buy you a mimosa!" He knew I liked mimosas. But he was a Bloody Mary type of guy and liked extra spice in his drink. And extra vodka.

I rolled out of bed. I brushed my teeth, showered, slipped on my favorite black v-neck, gray hoodie, and worn-out jeans, and was out the door. When I backed out of my driveway, I checked the mailbox and pulled out the usual collection of coupon deals and credit card notices (though I've never owned a credit card). I laid it all in the passenger seat, on top of the letter from Nashville, and drove to Coogie's.

❧

I was a few minutes early, but no big deal. I parked between a Mercedes convertible and a fancy SUV, and decided to take the letter with me to read until Oz arrived. Everything inside Coogie's was yellow or tan. The carpet was decorated with triangles that reminded me of slices of pizza. The air was filled with burning canola oil from the hash browns frying.

The waiter, a college student dressed in a simple polo shirt and jeans, seated me outside on the terrace that was hedged in by six-foot tall junipers for privacy. Locals filled all the tables except two, and they all wore summer shirts and sunglasses. You can always tell a local in Malibu. They look and dress like something between a hobo and a retired movie producer. Rarely clean shaven. Loose fitting clothes. Hair messy. And always–always– sunglasses.

I told the waiter to bring two waters and that we'd order soon. After he left, I pulled the opening of my hoodie closer to ward against the morning coastal chill. I pulled out the letter from Nashville. I read it once, then a second time, deciphering all the lawyer jargon.

Oz skipped over and we gave each other a bro-hug. That's a soft chest bump and a quick pat of each other's back. Oz was wearing his usual white t-shirt, crisp jeans, and Adidas sneakers. Blonde hair cut close, an athletic boxer's frame, and aviator sunglasses hiding his crystal blue eyes. "Good to see you," he said. He was his energetic self, like he had just worked out, showered, and downed a banana with a tall glass of fresh-squeezed orange juice. I say that because that really is probably what he had just finished doing, and all before 8 a.m. on a Saturday.

To better describe him, Oz's real name is Brian. He grew up in inner-city Tuscaloosa, Alabama, and had trained mixed martial arts (MMA) fighters at his uncle's dojo. Oz met his wife Shannon in New York City during an MMA expo fight, and since she attended Pepperdine, Oz followed her there. He became roommates with Finn and me after we found him sleeping in the library because he couldn't afford student housing.

He got his tuition paid because he applied as a theology student from Ireland. He mailed an envelope of letters to Dublin and paid some freelancers there to drop those enclosed letters into the mail to Pepperdine. Guinness Beer was awarding full-tuition scholarships to students of theology from Ireland if they wanted to study at Pepperdine, as long as they returned to Ireland once they graduated. This was because the company owner, Os Guinness, was a Christian and a huge fan of Pepperdine. So that's how Brian got the nickname "Oz."

It's a long story with a lot of comedy and drama, and you can read about it in Oz's memoir, *Alabama Irish*. But all that to say, we've been close friends since college. Oz and Shannon married after graduation, and both landed jobs on campus. She's a theater professor and Oz oversees the Study Abroad office.

"How's Shannon?" I asked him.

"She's good," he said as he flipped up the menu and scanned it. After two seconds, he knew what he wanted. Oz loved Coogie's. So much that he and Shannon were friends with the evening shift manager and often had him and his wife over for dinner. Oz knew everyone and liked everyone, until they gave him a reason not to.

The waiter brought Oz a Bloody Mary, and a mimosa for me. I sipped the mimosa and watched the bubbles rise from the bottom of the glass. Champagne always felt celebratory, and I wished Joanna and I had sipped more of it together when she was alive, celebrating every day that we had.

"So you said yesterday went well," he said. "What happened?"

I described my dinner with Dr. Willis. "So maybe things are going to change for the better," I went on. "I know I'll be here for the rest of my life, unless something drastic happens. And I'll be debt-free, for sure, pretty soon. This came in the mail." I handed the letter to him.

Oz opened and read it.

"Lawyer language. What's it say?"

"Remember when I used to tell you and Finn that I spent my summers in Tennessee? My grandmother Sandra, my dad's mom, had a vineyard in Franklin, outside Nashville. And a stone cottage home and a horse pasture. She used to let me do wine tastings when I wasn't even old enough to drive a car." I paused for a sip of the mimosa. "I haven't seen her since I was about fifteen. Now I wish I had kept in touch more, because she died two weeks ago."

"I'm sorry to hear that," replied Oz.

"I haven't talked to her in years. With Mom and Dad gone, I'm her only surviving relative. She's left everything to me. The vineyard, the cottage, everything."

"How much land?"

"Forty acres."

"Wow," Oz replied. "That close to Nashville, it'll be worth a lot." When the waiter returned, I ordered, and as Oz followed, I looked at the patrons surrounding us. They were all wealthy and I also knew that every single one of them wished they owned a retreat in the countryside. With that letter in my pocket, I felt a bit more important, knowing I would get the job I'd always wanted and be debt-free too.

I wondered how much the vineyard would bring in once I sold it. I looked across the sidewalk at Starbucks. Back in college, it was a Diedrich's Coffee, and Finn and Oz and I spent a lot of time together there. We would sit in its courtyard by a fountain that birds and children played in. I thought about the conversations we had and how my grandmother and her old-world sensibility had influenced me.

I lifted my glass to her in a silent toast. Why she had wanted to leave it all to me and not to one of her neighbors or vinedressers, I didn't know. Maybe she didn't purposefully leave it to me, I reasoned. Maybe she just passed away before writing her will.

Chapter 4

When the waiter returned with our food and the bill, Oz swiped it before I could look at it. "Brunch is on me," he said. "This calls for a celebration," and we clinked our glasses together. When Oz pulled a long draw from his Bloody Mary, swallowed, and ended with a loud, satisfied sigh, it reminded me of the edge he's always had about him. A love for whiskey and Guinness over Champagne and fine wine, though he did go to Napa once a year and bring home a few bottles of red from his favorite vineyard.

California had cultured him, but Oz was proof that you can take the boy out of Alabama but not take Alabama out of the boy. He could run, lift weights, and still spar with the students who came to him for private boxing lessons; he could also dress in a suit and discuss Plato. On Friday he could wear freshly shined shoes, on Saturday he could wear sneakers, and on Sunday he could wear cowboy boots, and on any of those days he would look completely in his element. He's one of the most interesting people I've ever known.

"So," Oz said. "You own a vineyard now, and land." Then he raised his glass again. "You're a gentleman," he said, pronouncing the word with exaggerated eloquence. "A scholar and a gentleman."

"Thanks." I chuckled at him.

"No, I'm serious. By eighteenth century standards, by owning land, you'd be considered a gentleman. Do you realize that? And you got the scholar down." I laughed at him, flattered and honored, but titles like that didn't really matter anymore. Oz continued, "So tell me about this place. I know a guy in real estate. Californians would love to get their hands on a vineyard outside Nashville just so they could brag to their friends about it."

I was silent for a moment, reliving some of my memories. "I remember the cottage, how Grandmother always had flowers planted at the front and to the sides. There was a porch where you could look out across the property. Butterflies and bumble bees were buzzing around on the flowers all the time. The cottage was built of rock, like something you'd see in a Kincaid painting. To the right was the vineyard and to the left was the horse pasture. Straight ahead was a yard and the road, and on the other side of the road there was some woods, with a creek where I used to swim. It emptied into a swimming hole and had a tree beside it with a rope swing."

"The vineyard stretched across all forty acres?"

"Yeah," I replied.

"Wow. A boutique vineyard for the family. Californians are gonna love that. How many bedrooms and bathrooms?"

"Two bedrooms, one that overlooked the property, which was Grandmother's. Two twin beds in the other room with a bathroom. Good kitchen with the living room in view. You know, no walls between them. That's about it, just a quaint little home. I wouldn't try to raise a family of more than four in it. But it was perfect for Grandmother and a guest."

"A weekend retreat," he affirmed. Oz folded his napkin in his lap, and we ate. He had an omelet filled with tomatoes, mushrooms, and spinach, and a glass of freshly squeezed orange juice. I had three scrambled eggs, two slices of bacon, one pancake with honey, and a glass of water.

"Any other facts you can give me?" he asked, chowing down.

"She had a shed on the side of her yard, designed like a barn. She kept the lawnmower in it. She used that on her small patch of yard. She had professional vinedressers tend to the vines. I think she shipped a lot of grapes in from California and they made the wine in Tennessee."

"That makes sense," Oz answered. "Tennessee isn't the ideal place to grow anything unless it's vegetables or watermelon. I get what you're saying. I'll need some photos. I'll send them to my guy and hear what he says."

After that, we finished our food and drinks and chit-chatted about everyday things. I caught Oz examining me every now and then, probably wondering what I was thinking. He knew I wouldn't move to Tennessee, but a part of him probably suspected I could be tempted into doing so. In my mind, I never would, not with all the history and memories of Pepperdine. Besides, how many people can say one of their best friends lives just down the street? As Grandmother would say, that's wealth.

I did wonder if the cottage would have shrunken, if the yard wasn't as big as I remembered, if some of the vineyard had been unkempt or portions replaced by a garden or something. I wondered if Grandmother's old desk, in front of her bedroom's bay window, was still there, or that old typewriter she used, or if the chimney still smelt of smoke from the previous winter.

"When are you going down to look at the property?" he asked.

"I'll probably find a weekend. With summer classes and all, I'll have to hurry back."

"It'll be a good break for you," he said. "Even if it's just for the weekend. Reminiscing about childhood memories may put some pep in your step. You haven't really been anywhere in a while." I knew he meant that I hadn't been anywhere since Joanna passed away, and he knew I knew, but there are some things that don't have to be mentioned again over a friendly, cheerful, and now sunny brunch in Malibu.

On Monday morning, after a full body workout at the gym on campus, I thought about all that had happened over the weekend: Finals being over, the opening for Chair, the vineyard, getting out of debt, Oz offering his real estate connections. I found myself thinking of Tennessee and I hummed the song "Wagon Wheel" by Old Crow Medicine Show as I popped down to the Malibu Market for a fruit and protein smoothie. I took the letter from the lawyer and a book by Emerson and sat at a picnic table in the park near the swing sets. There's something comforting about being surrounded by locals in a good mood, and seeing children playing and laughing.

I figured my next steps would be to contact the law office in Nashville, set up an appointment, and buy my plane ticket. The best time to go away for a weekend would be before the summer semester started.

I took out the letter and called the Tennessee number, and a young woman's voice answered the phone.

She didn't sound like one to waste time. The voice, which said she was Kim Satterfield's assistant, put me on hold twice after learning I was Sandra Lockwood's grandson. After some back and forth, a meeting was set in Nashville. I could fly in on Friday to visit the vineyard, have the meeting with her on Saturday, walk around the town of Franklin on Sunday, and then fly home on Monday.

When I told Oz of my plans, he said he wanted to join me, and that we should call Finn and see if he could go, too. I thought that was a great idea, so we coordinated dates and times and booked our flights. We would all arrive in Nashville on Friday evening and they would leave on Sunday. "One day is better than none," Finn had noted, and Oz agreed. I called Michael Young, the head vinedresser at Grandmother's vineyard. Ms. Satterfield had provided me with his name and number. I had planned on staying at a bed and breakfast, but after I shared our plans with him, Michael insisted we stay in Grandmother's cottage.

So everything was set.

That week, I finished loading all the grades into the database, and while professors and their families headed up to NorCal for quick vacations or to see family, I packed for Nashville.

On Thursday evening, with our flight leaving the next day, I poured myself the last glass of Pinot Noir. When Joanna passed away I found my escape through exercise and a lot of Guinness. Drinking a pint of beer with people I liked cheered me up, the warmth of it. But when one beer a week with friends turned into two beers a day no matter who was around, followed by the craving for more, I stopped. It scared me that I didn't have better control. I then began to understand how the depressed became alcoholics.

With the glass of wine in hand, I walked to the kitchen window and gazed across the ocean at the moon's milky trail. To the left stood the canyons and valleys with the city lights sparkling like a million stars. Now, they all looked a bit different to me. Not in a bad way. Just different. Maybe I was already being transformed by the new, exciting experiences over the past week. Since losing Joanna, it seemed to be the first time that I began to feel excited about life again.

Tomorrow, Oz and I would meet at the BNA airport

in Nashville, I would see some old stomping grounds, sleep in the house where I spent my childhood summers in, and see what the journey might bring. Life was getting better. At least I hoped it was.

Chapter 5

Oz and I waited on Finn at the rental car lounge. We rented two mid-sized cars in separate names since he and Finn were leaving a day earlier. I had decided to wear my black business suit with the usual crisp white dress shirt. I left the tie at home and unlatched the top two buttons to let me breathe. Oz sported his usual sunglasses, crisp dark jeans, sneakers, and for this trip he had added a navy blue-and-white-checkered dress shirt. His sleeves were rolled up to his elbows.

When Finn walked in, we exchanged handshakes and hugs. It was good to see him again. I hadn't seen him since the previous October when he and Eden came out for Pepperdine's Homecoming. Finn was always dressed as a gentleman, or like a professor straight out of Oxford. With chestnut brown hair and hazel eyes, he wore an almond-brown dinner coat, jeans, and brown penny loafers. Finn had grown up on a farm as an orphan, under the care of his grandfather. Finn was known for his old soul and he was usually more comfortable in the presence of the elderly than his own peers. When he was a toddler, his parents and older brother were killed in a car accident. Finn never really knew them, except through photos and stories.

I believe that's one of the things that forged our friendship. We were all, in some fashion, much like orphans.

After we all looked over each other for subtle changes, Finn said it was good to see me smiling again, and I was reminded that life is always better and easier when your best friends are at your side. I needed a break from Malibu. I knew that. And I needed to spend it with my friends. Life doesn't wait for us in our times of sorrow, I had learned.

Nashville was pretty much as I remembered, but once we made our way south to Franklin, and passed through Brentwood and Cool Springs, I realized how much had changed in the more rural places. The area had grown so rapidly that two towns had become one, joined by those relocating from California and New York because of Tennessee's relaxed tax laws.

Brentwood had become a series of clusters of neighborhoods and shopping malls, while Cool Springs had gotten posh, with modern buildings surrounded in its once-small financial district. All the while, Franklin still remained isolated, its own town… you know, two or three cattle farms between them.

When we turned on the road to approach the vineyard, the past kept returning. Memories of lying under oak trees and dreaming of traveling the world, swimming in the creek, catching lightning bugs in pickle jars, watching the deer and rabbits munching in the fields at dawn, and riding the bicycle Grandmother had kept for me. She'd give me pocket change and I would ride to downtown Franklin and buy an ice cream from a chocolatier.

Then I saw the vineyard from a distance. It was just as I remembered, but with some additions. An iron gate, which had been added since I was gone, stood open with a panoramic view of the vineyard stretching up the hill. At the top stood a shop, built like a lodge, overlooking everything. On the wrap-around deck and hillside, families and couples sat on blankets and at picnic tables, enjoying their wine and lunches. There must have been two hundred people there.

I rolled the windows down to take it all in. I could hear the birds singing and smell the honeysuckle. In front of the iron gate, pots of yellow and purple perennials sat atop bales of hay.

In the distance, to the left of the shop, at the farthest hill, my favorite oak tree still stood. Picnic tables sat beneath it for the customers, but otherwise it was just as I remembered. When I was a kid, I would lie under that tree and stare up through its branches and foliage, and dream about countries I'd explore one day. Often times I'd sit against its trunk and watch the rows of grapevines winding and disappearing over the hills. Blue skies, pastures, and lakes sat as an eternal backdrop. It was my piece of heaven.

The staff directing the vineyard traffic wore polo shirts, jeans, and carried walkie-talkies. They guided us towards two empty parking spaces, just inside the gate. At a closer look, the wine shop, with the wrap-around deck, was built with a wooden rail and clear plastic tarps rolled to the top, to be dropped to keep guests warm in the winter time.

A chimney had been built on the deck against the stone wall where, during the winter, people could enjoy their drinks by a warm fire.

When we stepped out of the cars, Oz and Finn could not stop talking about how incredible the place looked and how lucky I was. Half-jokingly, they said I should keep it as a great retreat for us all.

As we walked up the hill and toward the shop, a new tent and music pavilion stood to the side. I liked that. Between them and the shop stood a trellis whose rafters hung with ivy and sunset-pink blossoms. Lights the size of tennis balls dangled from the rafters to provide an ambiance at night.

So, over time, Grandmother's little vineyard had evolved into both a fully-fledged business and a retreat for Nashvilleans.

I didn't call Michael Young, the head vinedresser, until we were out of our cars and walking up the driveway, but still he met us on the shop's porch. He looked retirement age, though he seemed like the type to never retire. His head full of charcoal hair was slicked back, longer than most men's hair, and tucked behind his ears. He wore jeans and work boots and the sleeves of his cotton knit shirt were rolled up tight. We all shook hands and then he slicked the sides of his hair back, a gesture I later realized he unconsciously made when he was nervous or in deep thought.

He asked about our flight and we talked about how pretty the property looked. His eyes shone with pride as he boasted that all the renovations were his ideas and that the construction was funded by cash instead of loans.

I decided to stay quiet about my upbringing there and how exciting it was to be back. A part of me was afraid to be too open with him because we didn't know each other. As silly as it sounds, I didn't know how he might use that knowledge against me, and I also didn't want to grow close to him or anyone else who worked there. I knew I had to sell the vineyard, and the new owners might have their own vignerons and vinedressers, which meant his family would probably have to leave.

Michael led us inside the wine shop where more staff hustled and bustled. They opened the refrigerators along the walls and straightened the rows of wine bottles on display. Others counted cash at the register. A hostess took names and announced wait times while people lined up along the bar, enjoying the wine tastings. Three bartenders were popping bottles open and plopping empty ones into green recycle bins.

The smell of paint and lemon-polished dark oak floors still lingered from the shop's recent remodeling. Aromas of wine-soaked corks took me back to all the visits to various vineyards throughout the years. No matter which vineyard you visit, they all smell the same.

In the back corner stood shelves filled with various trinkets for sale. Everything from wine glasses to corkscrews, and a dozen other items with the Franklin Vineyard logo (a black circle with a silver F in the classical Roman style).

"Most of the workers here are students," Michael said, turning to us. "They attend Middle Tennessee State University. We also have interns from UC Irvine. They grew up in California and have never left the west coast. So they love an excuse to spend a summer or two here. They find it interesting that Civil War heroes are still honored here and battleground cemeteries are parks."

"I didn't realize wine could be grown in Tennessee," Oz said.

"Oh, sure, it can," Michael said. "But it's not always that good." Michael meant it as a joke, and we all shared a small laugh. "What I do is I order vines from UC Irvine and sometimes even their grapes to blend with what we grow here. Some Merlots, Cabernets, and Pinot Noirs. Those are our best. Sure, some Syrahs and Malbecs, and we even have the white wines, but the Tennessee palate is different. People like more of a fruity taste here."

Michael explained that the practice also provided financial support to UC Irvine's grape program. In return, Michael received interns and kept thriving relationships with the college professors. Michael said he even visited them once a year to talk shop and keep the relationships alive.

As our eyes scanned the room, one of the bartenders, who I hadn't noticed before, glanced over at me and our eyes caught. She was pretty with a firm jaw. In her mid-twenties, her silky cocoa-brown hair was wrapped in a messy knot held secure by an elastic band. With her hazel eyes, accented and profound against her dark features, she reminded me of a young business woman. She carried her shoulders straight, smiled at the guests, and laughed at the right moments. Certainly no one's fool.

She was the first to look away. When she did, the young woman beside her, a natural blonde with a slender face, light eyes, and high cheek bones bit back a smile and turned her attention back to the wine tasters. The blonde had seen what happened. She wore an engagement ring, and both young women kept Finn, and Oz, and me in their peripheral vision.

Michael's wife, Evelyn, popped in through a swinging door behind the bar. She had a motherly figure and red hair that she kept pinned up and out of her face. Michael waved her over and the two young women behind the counter ambled over with her.

"These are my wife and daughters," Michael said, introducing us. We all shook hands. The blonde was Julie and the brunette was Rachel. "Julie's the office manager," Michael continued. "And Rachel helps a lot. She's a waitress in Arrington, mostly." Arrington was a crossroads on the east side of Franklin, with only a caution light.

Finn and Oz were naturals with the Young family, exchanging all the southern pleasantries with energy, charm, and eloquence. I tried to keep my focus on Michael and the business. I would have handled myself differently if I could do it over again, but I wasn't there to make life-long friends.

Finn and Oz probably knew what I was feeling, so they stoked the fires of conversation to help keep the peace. They asked about what wood was used to construct the rafters, why these grapes were raised at the vineyard versus the ones that were shipped in.

When an attendant pulled Michael away with a question, our group fell silent until Rachel spoke up. Our eyes met again, but she directed her first question to Finn.

"What do you think of Franklin?"

"I love it!" he said. "I grew up outside Leiper's Fork."

"We know where that is," Rachel declared. "For a long time, there wasn't even a stop light there. We used to go horseback riding out at the Blackwell's farm."

"Yeah!" Finn answered. "I remember where that is."

"Where do you live now?" she asked.

"In Colorado, with my wife."

"I've been to Breckenridge," Julie said. "It's beautiful there."

Rachel stole a glance at me, but I dropped my eyes.

"It is," he replied. "I don't get out much... I mean, I do get out, just, not over to Leiper's Fork." Finn chuckled at himself, stammering over his words. "It was once my home, but not so much anymore… I mean, I don't dislike the place, don't get me wrong."

"You'll have to forgive Finn," Oz said, rescuing him. "He gets nervous around beautiful women."

Julie's cheeks went pink, and Rachel let out a small chuckle.

"Ryan's the real adventurer," Oz said, patting me on the shoulder and smiling at me. I knew what he was doing, and he knew I knew. Friends know when you're trying to set them up with someone. "You've traveled more than all of us," Oz went on, exaggerating. No one that we knew had traveled more than Finn. "He's quite the explorer," Oz added, looking at Rachel and smiling.

"I wish I traveled more," Julie confessed, "But there's always so much going on here."

"Yeah, I know, right?" Finn added. "I'm the same way! Colorado Springs won't let me leave. When your home gets ahold of you, look out!" Finn threw his hands up, all animated, which made Julie giggle.

About that time, a jazz band started outside. A bass, a saxophone, and lead guitar. Finn just couldn't resist. "I'd love to see the band," he said to Julie. "Can we?" he asked.

"You want me to show you?" she answered, looking happy to oblige. Finn nodded and the two headed out the door. Oz took that as an opportunity to leave me alone with Rachel. He stepped to Michael's side and started asking questions about why some of the bottle's bottoms were deeper than others, and how Michael decided on the design of the logo and labels. I'm sure Oz did have a slight curiosity regarding the branding, but I think he was more interested in seeing how I'd do with Rachel.

"Do you like jazz, Dr. Lockwood?" Rachel asked me, when she realized Oz wasn't coming back.

"You can call me Ryan," I replied, smiling small to be polite, but trying not to lead her on. "I do like jazz, but not when it's elevator music." That last word came out strong, like maybe I hated their jazz band. I didn't mean it that way, though I think that's how Rachel took it because her eyes made a quick scan of the room as if looking for an escape.

The awkwardness between us grew thicker with each passing second, so when Rachel spotted her mom talking with an assistant and pointing at a clipboard of papers, she found her excuse. "Well, it was nice meeting you, Ryan," she said. I nodded, and Rachel sped off, glad to get away from me.

Relieved and regretful all at once, I found distraction by browsing all the trinkets until Oz tapped my shoulder and we walked outside to find Finn. He was with Julie in front of the stage, and they were talking to a lanky college student. Finn was in full-energy mode, asking questions.

Rachel appeared soon after, strolling through the throng of people, checking on things. Did all the guests have enough to drink? Had anyone dropped and broken a glass? Did someone leave a mess from a picnic? She found Wanda, an assistant manager, and helped her clean off two picnic tables. The women didn't notice Oz and me standing a few feet away.

"This is great!" Finn said, as he bounded over to us. "A fantastic place and people. You don't want to get to know the locals?" he asked me. All Finn received in response was a shrug. "Lots of cute girls," Finn added. "Especially Michael's daughters."

"I'm not interested," I answered. And then I put my

foot in my mouth. "If women aren't happy, they run off. If they are happy, they die. It's a lose-lose situation." I looked away from Finn, only to see that Rachel and Wanda had heard every word.

Evelyn, after having three glasses of wine, grabbed Julie's hand and dragged her over to us, and motioned Rachel to join. "Hi boys," Evelyn said, cheerfully. "Have you had a chance to get to know my daughters?"

"Absolutely!" Finn answered, all enthusiasm. "Good people, and this place is great. Very alive."

"We love it here," Evelyn replied. That part bit me hard because I was reminded that when I sell the place, the new owners might fire them. "It's a couple's spot. People meet and fall in love here all the time. It's like an upscale Tinder."

"Mom," Rachel coughed, her eyes widening. Julie's face flushed tomato-red, and her eyes fell. Finn and Oz laughed, while I drew an impatient breath and looked away. Rachel saw my reaction, and by her expression it looked like she wanted to crawl into a hole.

"Oh, the girls don't like to admit stuff like that," Evelyn replied, never blinking. "But the people who come here are more upper class. It's not like a bar. The girls started working here when they were fifteen, and nice young men approach them all the time."

"But we grew out of caring about that," Rachel interrupted. "We learned quick that we needed to get to know them before we gave out our phone numbers."

Oz, understanding her intent to stifle Evelyn, followed Rachel's lead. "There's the chance that the good guys might never see you again," Oz said. "So, Rachel, how do you make it work with guys these days? I ask because the three of us have been out of the dating game a long time."

"People figure it out," Rachel replied, cutting off her mother, who had drawn a quick breath to answer. "If they want it bad enough."

Julie saw her chance, and looped her arm through Evelyn's. "Mom, would you show me how to play this song on your piano?"

"Yeah!" Evelyn returned, delighted. So they headed off toward their home on the nearest edge of the vineyard.

"I'd like to see how that's possible," I said to Rachel, startling those around me, given all my silence. "You can't leave people guessing what you want."

Rachel didn't let my comment faze her. "Well in the end, it might not matter," she answered. "Especially if all we do is get divorced or die off."

With that, she cast me a shining smile, and rejoined Wanda who was restocking the shop refrigerator. Now I admit, that wasn't my greatest moment. If anything in this world has caused me trouble, it's been my lack of patience and my mouth-running.

Chapter 6

Later that evening, just after the sun had set, Finn, Oz, and I unloaded our cars at Grandmother's cottage on the opposite side of the vineyard. A cobblestone path led to the same red front door I remembered, as well as the holly bushes at all four corners of the home. A white dogwood towered behind two redbud trees beside the kitchen window. A side patio overlooked the vineyard, and two chimneys sandwiched the home. I wished I could have seen Grandmother's home in winter, with everything powdered in snow.

Inside, the windows were open and the house smelled spring-fresh. The living room, dining room, and kitchen were all in view, with the bedrooms and two bathrooms down the hallway, just as I remembered. New cream tile adorned the kitchen walls above matching marble countertops, and cherry oak cabinets stretched to the ceiling, accenting a new silver stove. Some remodeling had obviously taken place.

In the living room, a maroon rug was encircled

by a leather couch, recliner, and a rocking chair that I had never seen before. There was no television–only a fireplace, and next to it a bookshelf stocked with novels, children books, and a set of 1986 black leather Encyclopedia Britannicas. Now those, I remembered.

On the fire mantel stood framed pictures of Grandmother and her sister, who had passed away before I ever got a chance to know her; a photo of me at eight years old, on the bicycle Grandmother had given me; and one of me as a baby in the arms of my mom, while she sat in a chair with Dad standing at our side, proud.

I strode straight to the back bedroom, Grandmother's room, while glancing into the room on my left and the bathroom on my right, allowing the old memories to play. The guest bedroom felt inviting, with matching twin beds that had light bedspreads with flower designs and hand-stitched pillows. Nightstands held Victorian lamps painted with images of eighteenth century gentlemen kissing maidens' hands.

In Grandmother's room was her old king-size bed with a cherry-oak frame, and matching dresser and desk. The desktop was solid dark oak, just as I remembered, with her leather swivel chair nestled in the footwell, still in great condition. I dropped my suitcase on the floor beside the bed, and set my laptop on the desk.

The breeze whispered through the window screens, lifting the long linen curtains that hung to the ground. It was all so familiar to me.

A silver lamp stood on the back corner of the desk top. A neat stack of bank statements sat to the side, which

Evelyn had left for my review. When I stepped back into the kitchen, Finn and Oz were tearing through the fridge and cabinets. Apples, oranges, and bananas sat in a bowl on the counter, compliments of Evelyn. Oz found fresh cartons of milk and eggs, and a pack of peppercorn bacon. "They stocked the fridge for us!" he called over his shoulder.

In the pantry, Finn found pancake mix, a jar of local honey, and cans of vegetables. He took inventory of all the cooking utensils and pots and pans.

I opened the hall closet and found some men's clothes that had probably belonged to a suitor: dress shirts, pants, jeans, leather loafers, two reasonably stylish suits, but with ugly brown and tan striped neckties draped across their necks. Standard 1960's fashion. I measured them against my size. The waists were an inch too large, but would work with a belt. The coats were a bit too loose in the armpits and on the sides, but could pass without an inspector's eye. Some of them, I wouldn't have worn except to a Halloween party.

As Finn and Oz kept prowling, I stepped out onto the patio where the last traces of the vineyard met the neighbor's wooden fence and horse pasture. The crickets and tree frogs had awakened, singing their timeless songs. Across the horizon, I saw the lightning bugs dip and flash. Off to the side, a plastic tan garden shed with green trim and a matching green roof stood in place of the old red barn I had played in as a kid. I wondered what had happened to it.

I spotted that old baby-blue metal table with the sap-stained fiber glass top. Most of the paint had flicked off, exposing a rusty base. It sat on the patio, leaning against the house. The old white plastic chairs that I remembered were gone. I wondered if they had rotted or broke apart. Grandmother and I used to sit there and watch the sun go down.

This spot was where she let me taste her wines and help her decide which ones to sell the following year. At the end of every summer, Grandmother would present me with a tray of shot glasses filled with six different reds and whites. A private wine tasting for a twelve year old. I would name my favorites. She valued my opinions since I didn't drink wine except with her, and she knew I'd be honest. We never told my parents. I loved that we kept it a secret.

I loved my parents, and I know they loved me, too, but I always had to fight for their attention. When I wasn't in boarding school, I spent only May and the last half of December at their home, seeking their affection, while June and July were given solely to the joys of being in Tennessee.

Grandmother acted more like an older sister, and sometimes even a peer. There really were no strict rules like bedtime and what I could or couldn't watch on TV. In her home in the 1980s, there were only four channels, and were all family-friendly. The Andy Griffith Show came on every day at 6 p.m., followed by the news, and that was pretty much the extent of our TV watching. Grandmother talked to me like I was a young adult, treated me like one, and she even let me "drink." It makes me laugh to think back on it all.

When Grandmother stayed inside to do chores, or escape the summer humidity, I played in the vineyard, which felt to me then like a labyrinth. There, I could pretend to be a spy, a solider in the trenches, or a hero out to rescue a girl I loved from a horrible dragon.

Grandmother kept a bicycle for me in the barn, a white Schwinn with red italic writing. Between the vineyard, the creek, the rope swing and nearby downtown Franklin, my summer was set. If a few friends my age had joined me, the summer might have been even more fun, but I was just fine there with Grandmother.

Downtown Franklin, as I remembered it, was a picturesque grid of homes built in Colonial and civil-war era Victorian styles. There were boutiques, cafés, pubs, coffee shops, a restored 1920s theatre, and centuries-old churches whose bells still chimed at noon. Families strolled the sidewalks at all times of the day. As a kid, I loved riding my bike there in the early '80s, when life was simpler and I wasn't surrounded by bickering and squabbling adults.

When I woke from my little daydream, I was still looking at the old weather-stained table when images of Rachel came to me. I saw her standing behind the shop counter, and then I saw the shock on her face at hearing my rude remarks. I didn't intend to cause her pain, but I reasoned that I'd soon have the property settled and return to my life in California, and I could put all of this behind me.

The afternoon sun was starting to sink as I shook out

the memory of her, stepped off the patio, and headed to the shed, curious about what might be inside. I found a John Deere riding lawn mower that couldn't have been more than three years old. I remembered the old Snapper that once sat there.

I found the rusty toolbox that Grandmother always left open, still sitting on the same shelf. I walked over and sifted through some of the tools and found her old ratchet. She used to ride the Snapper mower up onto cement blocks so that she could lie down underneath it and change the blades. At twelve years old, I wanted to help, so she let me give it a shot.

One time, the nuts had been stripped, making them impossible to remove. A hacksaw was probably in order, but we'd have to leave to buy one at the Dollar General Store. After a while, nothing was working as I expected, and the air was hot and stuffy. The sweat kept seeping into my eyes and stinging them. I fumbled with the ratchet and dropped it for the ninth time. When I raised my head to see where one of the nuts had fallen, I banged my head on the blade guard. I launched to my feet and threw the ratchet across the shed. It crashed against the wall.

"Why can't you just get another one?" I yelled, meaning the lawn mower.

"You got the money to buy another one?" she retorted. I lifted the pouch of my t-shirt and wiped my forehead, to remove the sweat and dirt. "Let's take a break," Grandmother suggested, sliding off her garden gloves and patting my shoulder. "It's time for lunch anyway." While walking together, she said to me, "I know the work isn't easy, but remember: no matter what happens to us in life, we decide how to respond."

I smiled at the memory, turned the old ratchet over in my hands, then plopped it back into the toolbox. On the other side of the shed I noticed a tarp hiding something. When I looked under it, I found a four-wheeled Gator in great condition. "Well, look at you, Grandmother," I muttered. I checked the dashboard and it had a full tank of gas with only 150 miles on the odometer. I'll have to ride that later, I thought.

Dusk was setting in, so I returned to the cottage. When I went inside, Finn and Oz were eating sandwiches. Sliced meats and cheeses, tomatoes, mustard, and mayonnaise were scattered across the countertop. "How was the walk?" Finn asked, taking a bite.

"Really cool," I replied. "A lot like I remember, but everything's smaller."

"Does Rachel remind you of someone?" Finn asked. "We think we've seen her somewhere."

"She did look familiar," added Oz. "She didn't go to Pepperdine, did she?"

I shook my head at them, wondering if they were simply talking about Rachel for my sake, but I didn't want to think about her. You know, her gorgeous slender face and nose with that silky cocoa hair and matching eyes. Nope, I sure didn't.

"She's cute," Oz said, directing his remark toward me. I smirked and refused to respond. Instead, I ate a sandwich and we talked and laughed at old stories. Finn shared tales from Colorado. Oz talked about his and Shannon's adventures in Italy and Ireland. I laughed with them but the laughter was different from what it once was. Life can do that. Change your laughter.

It occurred to me in the kitchen that I hadn't been filled with the same energy as I once had. That person who had been married to Joanna, young and healthy and in love, with a fulfilling job and friends living just down the street. That person and those times were gone. I wouldn't have admitted it at the time, but despite the laughter on the outside, deep down, I left like a part of me was slowly wasting away.

⌘

The next morning, I woke to the sun shining through the trees, lighting up Grandmother's bedroom. To my great comfort I remembered that my best friends were sleeping in the room beside me, and that I was back in a place I had once called home. Memories of Joanna came, and for the first time in my life I regretted that I had never brought her to Tennessee. She loved Napa and Sonoma, the grandeur of the vines, and the musty and rusty smell of all the cellars we toured. Life is short, I reminded myself.

I turned onto my opposite hip, shut my eyes, pulled the covers over my head, returning to that familiar place where I dwelt on my loss and sadness, but then I heard Finn and Oz joking in the kitchen. Someone was pulling out all the pots and pans, and I could smell coffee brewing, so I rolled out of bed, basking in the comfort of the sunshine and the sound of my friends' laughter.

I stepped into my Pepperdine shorts, slid on my t-shirt from the night before, and walked into the kitchen. Finn had already showered and was dressed for the day, but Oz was in his boxers and had puffy eyes. Finn was reciting a list of items they needed from the grocery store, and Oz was typing them into his phone. I said my good mornings and the guys were all smiles. Finn handed me the cream and a coffee mug. He knew I liked to put the cream in first, then the coffee on top. No sweetener. Good friends know how you like your coffee.

Finn and Oz said they had slept well and that they'd whip up a great breakfast. When Oz was nineteen, he had enlisted his aunt to teach him how to cook, because he had met Shannon on a trip to New York and wanted to impress her. When I asked if they needed help, they said no, so I decided to go for a morning walk.

Normally I would have stayed and chatted with the guys, but I was still thinking about Joanna and why I had never returned to Tennessee. It was bothering me. Also, I was feeling guilty for not staying in touch with Grandmother after I left for college. I poured my coffee, said I'd be back in a bit, and stepped out the door.

From the patio, I made my way through the furthest leg of the vineyard and ambled along the neighbor's fence where Arabian horses grazed among the clover and daffodils. The wild violet annuals jiggled on their vines at every gust of wind, and Monarch and canary-yellow butterflies bounced between the blossoms. On the far side of the pasture, at the edge of the woods, I caught a glimpse of a rabbit sniffing along the tree lines. When it saw me, it scampered off.

The old narrow trail my bicycle had once cut along the fence was gone. When I was about nine years old, at that exact spot, I heard Grandmother yell, "Ryan!" and I had slammed on the breaks, twisting and turning my bike to a sliding halt, throwing up a rooster tail of grit and grass. I turned and looked back to the patio. Grandmother was standing next to the table and chairs; they were still new back then. She held up half of a watermelon that had been sliced right down the middle. Its gorgeous red fruit shone in the sun. A salt shaker and two plates awaited us on the table. "I cut the watermelon!" I could hear her yelling.

A deer leapt across the pasture on the opposite side from the horses, waking me from thoughts of forgotten days. I stepped over to the fence and leaned on it, crossing my arms over the top rail to watch the grass wave. Peace and restfulness were the only words that came to mind. A world before Joanna. Before Pepperdine.

I had forgotten how much I missed simple beauties like the dew, and the morning mist hovering over the pasture. Now that I was a man, I began to understand how much Grandmother cared for me, and how hurt she must have been that I never called or wrote, let alone visited.

My phone buzzed in my pocket. It was a text from Finn saying breakfast was ready, so, I made my way back to the cottage. When I reached for the side door, I caught a whiff of made-from-scratch biscuits, and when I entered, I saw Finn, Oz, Julie, and Rachel sitting at the dining table.

Chapter 7

They were eating a delicious spread, more food than Oz and Finn could've prepared during my walk: scrambled eggs, bacon, sausage, hash browns, pancakes, toast, orange juice, milk, and of course the biscuits. Clearly the sisters had brought some of it. "There he is," Finn announced when I returned.

I couldn't ignore the fact that, when I saw Rachel, my spirit lifted. Her hair and those eyes and fine lips. She managed only a slight smile at me, then moved her attention back to the group. I figured that was best, and I couldn't blame her, especially given my behavior the night before.

The skeptic in me wondered if their making breakfast for us was a genuine gesture or a move steeped in manipulation. I believed the sisters liked Oz and Finn, but I knew Rachel hadn't taken to me very well, and I'm sure she had told Julie what I had said. Even if the display was to butter up the new owner of the vineyard, it didn't matter, I reasoned. The vineyard was still going to be sold, and that was that.

I passed behind Finn and Oz, and set my mug in the sink. "How was your walk?" Finn asked, looking over his shoulder at me.

"It was fine."

"They brought us breakfast," Oz said, as I washed my hands.

"I see that," turning back to everyone and smiling. "Thank you," I said to the sisters, and I could tell they knew I meant it. I wiped my hands on a dish towel.

"How did you learn to cook so well?" Finn asked the Youngs. I took a seat next to Finn and Oz, with the sisters across from us. Someone had left a plate and silverware out for me. The crew passed the food around to me, and I poured a glass of orange juice. Rachel kept her attention on Finn and Oz. I figured that if she was interested in me at all, she would want to see how I acted in the company of my closest friends, to see glimpses of my character. At least that's what I would have done if I was interested in a girl.

"Mom had us cooking since we were little," Julie answered. "She needed help, with everything going on at the vineyard."

Oz stole a glance at me, but I kept my eyes on my plate, moving the food from the fork to my mouth. I was a bit nervous, actually. An insecure side of me wondered what Rachel thought of me, or if Finn and Oz had said anything nice about me to them. "What are you up to today?" Oz inquired, interrupting my musings. I guess he didn't want to leave me out.

"Just running some errands," I replied. But I knew exactly where I was going, to the law office, and that fact would have been too touchy for the Youngs. "There's lots of stuff to see in Franklin," I added. "Then there's Nashville, but I think you guys will like Franklin better. Finn knows. He's been there," I went on, gesturing toward him.

"What else is there to do around here?" Finn inquired. "The place has changed."

"Go to the lake," Julie answered. "There's lots of outdoors stuff to do. Downtown Franklin's good, though, if you like coffee shops."

"The nightlife in Nashville's worth seeing," Rachel added. "Which I'm sure you know, but once you've seen it, that's it."

"It's worth seeing if you haven't been there before," chimed Julie.

"I'll take you to some places," Finn said to Oz. "I want to see some stuff before I leave."

"Where's a good place to read?" I asked. "Any favorite coffee shops or cafés?"

The sisters both looked at me, their eyes wide, probably surprised I was asking them something.

"Edison's," Rachel replied, curtly. "Do you know it?"

I shook my head no, and then looked back down at my plate. "It's a chic little lunch place," she continued, and I could tell by the direction of her voice that she was talking to Finn and Oz. "But it turns into a fine dining venue at night. Candlelight. That kind of thing." When

I looked back up at her, I saw her jaw clench. She was obviously watching me, though staring straight ahead.

"So, you're all married?" Julie asked us. She placed her elbows on the table and lifted her coffee mug closer to her mouth. Finn and Oz both wore rings, and with Julie's engagement ring–but not yet a wedding band– it was clear she was looking forward to marriage and excited to discuss it.

"I met my wife at Pepperdine," responded Finn. "So did Ryan." The words came out of Finn's mouth before he knew it. I saw a tinge of regret in his eyes after he said it, but I didn't let on. I just kept eating.

"I met mine in New York," Oz said, quickly. Probably to take away the attention he knew I didn't want. "We got married after we graduated."

"What about you two?" Finn chimed in, trying to help.

"We're divorced," Julie confessed, glancing at Rachel. Both sisters chuckled. "We were both too young."

"Dr. Lockwood?" Julie turned to me. "What's your story?"

"I was married, but life happened," I managed to say. I hoped they sensed that I didn't want to discuss it further. I had been prepared to answer that kind of question, but I wanted it left at that.

"I'm sorry," Julie offered. "Do you think you'll ever marry again?"

"Probably not," I stated, matter of factly.

"Why?" Rachel quizzed. Julie shot her eyes at

Rachel, obviously recognizing a certain tone. Rachel kept her eyes on me, stony; a small, unreadable smile moved across her lips.

I wasn't happy that I had hurt her with what I had said before, but I wasn't intimidated by her either. I knew what I believed when it came to marriage, and why I believed it. I taught society and culture classes on it: The History of Marriage and Marriage in the Modern World. A part of me was numb to women back then. Probably because I had loved two so deeply, and lost them both. Joanna–and my mom.

"Marriage was lovely in the beginning," I explained. "But I'm in a different chapter of my life now. Besides, I'm not in a hurry to get married again when there's a fifty percent divorce rate." When people get married, they don't believe they'll ever divorce, yet so many marriages fail. If I wanted my students to leave with anything from my classes, it was an understanding of the history and origin of marriage, and how it had evolved over time and across society. Then, the students could decide if marriage was right for them.

"And what will you do with your new chapter?" Rachel persisted. I knew she was probably talking about the vineyard and not my bachelorhood.

"Time will tell," is all I said, as if I was oblivious to what she meant. Rachel wanted to know the future of the property and her family, and I didn't blame her. I would have wanted to know too.

After that, Julie reminded Rachel that they needed to go to the store before opening the shop. So we all shook hands, exchanged thank yous, and we guys agreed to bring the washed dishes back to their house.

Chapter 8

After the sisters left, we cleaned the kitchen and then Oz took a shower while Finn skimmed through his newsfeed on his phone. I poured another cup of coffee and took a kitchen chair out onto the deck. I just wanted to be surrounded by the sights and sounds that had comforted me when I was a boy, so I unfolded the old table, brushed off the dust, and set my mug down.

I thought about all that had transpired between Rachel and me. Her reactions began to make more sense. She had been hurt by love, too, and her marriage had ended, probably badly. How many marriages end in peace?

As I sipped my coffee, I recalled how Dad once told me that most people are doing the best they can with what they know and what they have. People are just at different stages in their journeys. Part of being mature is understanding that, and showing patience, empathy, and compassion. Everyone has said and done things they later recognized as mistakes.

Dad's advice was always there, with me, everywhere

I went. But practicing those teachings, especially when I was depressed, was harder than I had imagined. "Easier said than done," as people say.

I remembered that first year of life without Joanna. When the mornings came I would wake and hope it had all been a nightmare. That Joanna wasn't really gone. That she and our child, which we planned to bring into the world, would be alive and healthy. But within a second of that early morning wake, I was reminded of the truth. That my parents, wife, and child were gone. I didn't have siblings, so I was alone at Pepperdine.

The only thing that kept me going was knowing my friends and students needed me, and I wanted to be a better example to them than to choose suicide. I never had been and I never would be a quitter.

"Get up, son! Get up!" Dad said to me, after I fell on the ice as a boy. It was the first year I learned how to skate. "You're not going to get anywhere lying down." And so I got up. "Get up!" I would yell at myself as I lay in bed in the mornings, without Joanna. "Get up!" And I'd pull myself up and out of bed with the same strength it would take a horse to pull a wagon. I would get up and get going, to meander through a world I considered worn out, broken, and torn.

I had read Viktor Frankl's book, *Man's Search For Meaning*, and it helped me. "Find a mission only you can accomplish. And surround yourself with loved ones," was the overall theme. So I made it my mission to teach literature the way only I could teach it. To not mimic other professors, but just be myself. Focus on the philosophy and parables of all the life lessons I taught my students throughout the years.

I surrounded myself with faculty and staff who cared about me, and I welcomed the efforts of Oz and Finn to be available. I made myself present to the students who came to see me. Often times the students visited my office not to talk about class, but to confide in me about the problems and crises in their lives, and to see if the professor had any advice or words of wisdom. "The wounded healer," as professor Henri Nouwen wrote. "Help others heal the wounds in their lives, those same wounds you have in your own. And through that, you'll find healing," was his teachings.

As an undergrad I admired the Oxford professor C.S. Lewis, who also lost his parents when he was young. Later in Lewis's life. Lewis married a woman with cancer, knowing she would die, because that's how much he loved her. I always admired that about him, though I never told anyone.

I had already struggled with mild depression before meeting Joanna. Dr. Decker, my physician back in Calgary. He recommended that I try a little medication, but I didn't want to and I never did. Later, when I was a junior at Pepperdine, I volunteered to help at freshman orientation, and that's where I met Joanna.

She was from an upper-class family of fine art dealers and traders in Manhattan. During high school, she volunteered every summer at an orphanage in the inner city, and she was intrigued to learn that I had worked with AIDS victims in Zambia the summer after my freshman year. Even though I was considered a "foreigner" from Canada to her New York parents, we fell in love and married.

Her love was the only drug I needed for my mild depression. I loved lots of things about Joanna. Her olive skin, how she tanned well after being in the sun for only a little while, and her dark hair against her emerald eyes.

I knew when I first met her that I'd never forget her. My life kicked into overdrive after we met, and in a good way. I was grateful to be alive, just so that I could spend more time with her. Just so that I could love her, which I believed meant being there for her and serving her, striving to put her needs above my own. Her love and respect for me was returned. Finn and Oz both said that in all their years they'd never seen a couple who complimented each other better than Joanna and I. We were together and we were happy.

On the weekends, Joanna and I would drive up the Pacific Coast Highway with Finn and Eden, and Oz and Shannon. The road wove through the green hills that rose into cliffs over the azure ocean. The sun was always shining in the only way the SoCal sun knows. The easy breeze was always breezing, and the happy sea gulls were always hovering, like kites.

We would stop and take photos at the lighthouses and taste the coffees and chocolates in the tiny shops in the quaint little towns along the way. Sometimes at night we'd all head into Santa Monica to the British and Irish pubs, but most of our evenings were spent on the beach by a fire. Finn knew a family who owned property near Point Dume, which allowed a panoramic view of the coast. We'd build our fire there, and huddle around it against the chilly coastal wind. We roasted marshmallows under a sky filled with a billion stars, with the moon's silver trail shimmering across the top of the ocean's black waters. Faint scents of sea salt and scorched timber filled our noses, and we felt as if we'd be young and alive forever.

I would often look at the firelight pulsating on the faces of my friends, all of them laughing, carrying on, and I'd see the wind curl Joanna's hair. I wondered if that's what heaven would be like, to be surrounded by loved ones before an eternal backdrop of beauty and grandeur.

On Sundays, after brunch, we'd often ride over to the bluffs at Westward Beach, an area few tourists visited. We'd sit on the ledges and drink wine we had bought in Napa Valley, while watching the sailboats rock their way to Marina Del Rey.

Joanna would lean into me and I would kiss the top of her head and breathe in the scent of her hair. Sometimes, she stuck a buttercup behind her ear, just to be silly, but she looked beautiful when she did it, and I always felt that hard, aching pulse in my throat. Her beauty moved me, and I was overwhelmingly grateful for it.

One day, I told them all, I would be the Department Chair in Literature here at Pepperdine. Joanna and I would be set and secure. She was proud of me for that goal and ambition, believed I could achieve it, and that made me feel good. We knew we'd never have to leave the place where we fell in love, unless we wanted to, and if Finn and Eden and Oz and Shannon ever left, they could always come back and have a place to call home. They would all smile and wink at me when I went on and on about my dreams, but they believed in me, and I was thankful.

"Hey Ryan," Finn said, interrupting. Finn stood at the door with his hands in his pockets. I hadn't heard him come out. "We're going to downtown Franklin. You wanna come before your appointment?"

"I'll have you guys drop me off at the lawyer's office, if that's okay. Then I'll meet up with you later."

"Yeah. For sure," Finn said, smiling back. He held the car keys in his hand and thumbed in the car's direction. "You ready?"

⌒⌒

Finn and Oz dropped me off in front of an eight-story glass building in the posh business district of Cool Springs, while they went off to explore the town.

Kim Satterfield's law office was on the first floor. The building smelled new, and the marble floors reminded me of money. In her suite, a young secretary with black-rimmed glasses sat behind a shiny oak desk with a bouquet of flowers sitting on the edge.

"Hi," the secretary said, looking up at me when I walked in. She had been typing at her computer.

"I'm here to see Ms. Satterfield."

In the back, down a corridor, stood a line of offices.

Over the secretary's left shoulder was Ms. Satterfield's office. Her heavy door stood open, revealing a newly carpeted floor. I heard the creaking of an office chair, someone standing, and Ms. Satterfield appeared around the corner to shake my hand.

Dressed in a gray pantsuit with a linen scarf, despite the warm weather, she wore fancy rings, bracelets, and a loose silver watch. She held a leather-bound folder with a collector's pen sticking out, and a pair of glasses hung from the front pocket of her jacket. She reminded me of a sixty-year old Diane Keaton, but with the energy of a college student.

"Hi Dr. Lockwood," she said, shaking my hand. Her smile was warm and her handshake was firm.

"Thanks for meeting on a Saturday," I answered tactfully.

Ms. Satterfield shooed the thought away with her hand. "We're always open on Saturdays," she dismissed with a smile. She led me into her office, where two acorn-brown leather chairs sat in front of her desk with a coffee table between them. A glass bowl was filled with silver foil-wrapped chocolates. She kept the folder closed and crossed her legs when she sat across from me.

"So, you're wanting to sell the property and return to your life," she said. She spoke directly but with empathetic eyes. "You know, the Youngs have been there for years. Have you thought about just letting them manage it while you receive the profits in California?"

"I have, but I'm not interested," I answered. "My life is at the university, and with my students and friends, I don't have time to worry about a vineyard."

"Have you thought about selling the vineyard to the Youngs?"

"I think you and I both know they couldn't afford it. Even with a loan."

"Well, perhaps you can have it for your summers or the weekends," she suggested.

"I live in Malibu. I'll enjoy my summers just fine."

"But–"

"I don't have any interest in owning a vineyard," I stated. "I don't have the time, and I want to keep my life simple." I was a bit taken aback by how unprofessional she was coming across. The sale seemed personal to her, and when I shifted in my chair, I think Ms. Satterfield sensed my concern. "How did you find me at Pepperdine?"

"Your grandmother knew you were there," she answered.

"I know that," I replied. Grandmother knew I had gone to college there and never left.

"And I knew her," Kim added, taking her glasses out of her pocket and looking down at them. "Lots of people loved her. Cool Springs is growing fast, but I grew up in Franklin, before everything was booming."

"Grandmother was a good woman."

"She was. She wasn't a vigneron, but she loved the people who came to her vineyard. She enjoyed sharing it with them."

I wondered if Ms. Satterfield was hinting that all my time in California had caused me to lose touch with what Grandmother would have wanted. That I no longer viewed life from a small-town traditional perspective, but saw life in terms of big cities and progressive values. I knew in my heart that Grandmother wouldn't have wanted me to sell the vineyard to outsiders and risk the Youngs being fired. She would've wanted it to stay in the family. Kim Satterfield knew it and I knew it, but I was sticking to my decision.

The idea of owning a vineyard did intrigue me a little, but I cared more about my freedom and my own dreams at Pepperdine. Besides, I was the guy who might enjoy reading books on a business development–not actually running one.

"Dr. Lockwood, Sandra cared about the Youngs, and the people in town. Lots of people loved her, too."

"I appreciate you saying that," I replied. "But you know what she liked more? Having a place in the countryside that overlooked a vineyard and drinking as much wine as she could handle. So, she hired people to do the grown-up work. Like trim the vines and handle the finances." Ms. Satterfield chuckled and looked back down at her glasses. Some of the tension eased. "So, you know the Youngs?" I asked, already suspecting she did.

"I do. It's a small town in a big city and not everyone has a vineyard."

"Well, Grandmother enjoyed being single and being with her friends, and I'd like to spend the rest of my life doing the same. The property's been appraised?"

Ms. Satterfield nodded, not bothering to hide a sigh of defeat while opening her folder. "Yes. Here," she offered, handing me the executive summary of the property's appraisal. I scanned it. "It's worth $880,000 for the property. That includes Sandra's cottage, the vineyard, everything. All debt-free."

"What about the Youngs' house?" I asked.

"It's theirs. They bought it from Sandra a few years back."

"Oh, so they won't be made to leave. They can stay."

"If they can afford to without an income," Ms. Satterfield replied. When I looked up at her, she dropped her eyes, knowing she shouldn't have said that. No room for emotion in business.

"How much is the wine bringing in each year?" I asked.

"After taxes and after the vine growers and distributors take their cut? About $10,000 a year."

"That's all?"

"It's not Napa Valley, Dr. Lockwood. Michael and Evelyn make $50,000 a year. That's why they don't live in a mansion."

"Then I'm definitely selling," I confirmed.

"What about the Youngs?"

"They won't be mistreated. I'll talk to the new owners and make sure Michael stays on as the vigneron."

"But that might not work," Ms. Satterfield replied. "You can't guarantee that, even if it's in the contract."

"I can be pretty persuasive," I answered.

"I know it's none of my business," she said, fidgeting with her bracelet. "But the Youngs are good people."

"I know they are," I said, coughing back a small

chuckle, as if I was selling the place to punish them. It wasn't personal. It was practical. "Is that all?" I asked. I was ready to go. When she nodded, I said I wanted time to look over the papers before signing. I shook her hand, headed out the door, and texted Finn and Oz. They were at McCreary's, a tiny Irish pub in downtown Franklin, that had a reputation for serving good Guinness and farm-to-table stew. On Saturday nights, an Irish quartet set up in the far corner and played traditional Irish music.

I was glad they had found the place. I called Michael Young while I waited for them, and set up a meeting at his home office for that afternoon. I wanted to tell him in person rather than over the phone. It would be more respectful that way.

However, I knew that breaking the news to him wouldn't be easy.

Chapter 9

Finn drove us back to the vineyard while I sat in the backseat, behind Oz. From the hilltops, the countryside looked like Ireland, with squares of greens and browns stitched together like a quilt. A robin's egg blue sky, white clouds–no gray.

I took a deep breath, absorbing the serene beauty. As my friends chatted and laughed in the front, just being there brought a peace I had long missed. "If only they would talk to one another and not to me," as C.S. Lewis wrote. He just enjoyed having his friends there after his wife passed, but he didn't want to engage in all the jokes and conversations.

Finn wanted to spend as much time with us as he could, so I invited Oz and him to join me to meet with Michael. When we rolled up to the vineyard, Rachel and Julie were sitting under the trellis. Climbing roses twined above them, with butterflies and bumblebees moving restlessly from bloom to bloom. A cool breeze kept the air pleasant and carried the scent of honeysuckle. Rachel's hair was pinned up and she was dressed in her restaurant attire. She was probably heading to work soon. They were talking and drinking iced sangria from Mason jars.

When we stepped out of the car, the sisters waved hello.

"Hi guys!" Julie yelled, seeming her usual charming self. Rachel smiled, but remained reserved.

"We were just talking about you two," Finn called back. That was true, but it was more in passing than anything. He and Oz had talked about how kind they were.

"What are you guys up to?" Julie called back.

"Ryan has a meeting with Michael," Finn returned.

Julie nodded and raised her glass as a toast to us. "Hope it goes well!" she said.

We smiled and nodded. My eyes met Rachel's but she slid them back to Julie. She didn't like me at all. I reached the door first, probably because I was walking faster than the others. It wasn't easy for me to face the sisters, given all that was happening.

"Just go on in!" Rachel called out as I reached for the door knob. "No need to knock." My back was to them, so I'm glad she didn't see my expression, but I wondered if she would have said the same if Finn or Oz had arrived at the door first. Her tone was nothing but hospitable, but well-timed words can mean plenty. Thankfully, when I twisted the door knob, Evelyn swung open the door and greeted us with her usual welcoming smile.

The aroma of ham and baked sweet potatoes filled the house, probably from lunch. Some windows were open and the air felt nice and cool. As in Grandmother's home, there were no walls between the living room, kitchen, and dining room. A simple recliner, couch, and one chair stood in a semicircle, facing a TV. There was a piano off to the right. The bedrooms were down a hall, while Michael's office sat on the opposite side. Family photos decorated the walls, showing the family of four growing up.

I thanked Evelyn for the stocked fridge, and Finn and Oz did the same, adding how nice the cottage looked and how welcome they felt. Evelyn beamed even more and shooed their compliments away. She said they were glad to have us. Michael emerged from his office and waved hello and shook our hands. His smile seemed forced when he greeted us. I smiled back, dutifully. I wondered if Ms. Satterfield had called ahead and delivered the news.

"We'll wait out here," Finn said, and Oz nodded in agreement. They understood the need for our privacy. They sat in the living room while Evelyn finished putting away the leftovers from lunch.

I followed Michael into his office, which probably had been a small bedroom at one time. A wooden desk, which could have been his great-grandfather's, had papers stacked and scattered across the desktop. An olive-green metal filing cabinet sat in the corner. Empty bottles of wine lined the windowsill, and I suspected that each bottle held a special significance.

Michael walked behind his desk to straighten some of the papers. "You can shut it if you want," he said, gesturing to the door. I closed it out of respect, but left it a crack open. I didn't want to come across as needing us to be too private, but I reasoned he might not want Evelyn or my friends hearing everything.

I told Michael that I had talked with Ms. Satterfield, looked over the documents, and stated my intentions: to seek out a buyer and negotiate in the contract that the Youngs were to stay on as vinedressers for at least three years. Michael kept his arms crossed while I spoke, and I knew it was his way of remaining cool and collected. Oz and Finn said later that they heard Michael's voice rise here and there, and each time they would steal a glance at Evelyn, but she didn't seem to hear it while clanking and clanging dishes.

"My wife and I have been here fifteen years," he said. "Your grandmother was like an aunt to us. I raised my daughters here!"

"I understand that," I replied. "I do. And I'll make sure to tell the new owners–"

"You know there's no guarantee," Michael interrupted, his voice just above a yell, and his hands spread like starfish, gesturing wildly. "This vineyard's in the shape it's in because of us. Your grandmother hired us for a reason. These vines are our life!"

"I know," I answered, trying to keep sympathy in my tone. "And no business man in his right mind would ignore what you've done. Only an idiot would get rid of you."

"There's lots of idiots out there!" Michael shot back.

"When I sell it, you and your family will be taken care of financially. You won't–"

"You think it's about the money? It plays its role, yes, but…" Michael stopped himself and hid his face with his hand. There was no sense in arguing, and he knew it. The decision had been made. Three years was a fair number for both parties. If the owners didn't like Michael, then they could let him go after the contract ended, and if Michael knew they wouldn't keep him, he would have plenty of time to make other plans.

I knew, despite Michael's fears, that he and his family were indispensable and that over time the new owners would realize the same. Not only were the Youngs personable, hardworking, and skillful, but they had a good business relationship with all their suppliers and distributors.

But from Michael's point of view, every day after those three years passed, their job security would remain uncertain. Every week, he, Evelyn, and their daughters would wonder if it was their last.

I remember shaking Michael's hand, and I remember his parting words: "It is what it is." And when I opened the door and left, with a glance over my shoulder, Michael was staring out the window with his arms crossed.

Evelyn turned and smiled at us as we passed behind her. I saw no judgment or accusation in her expression, just hospitality and kindness.

∽

When we arrived back at Grandmother's, Finn and Oz loaded their suitcases into the car, then returned to the house for a "dummy check," as Finn liked to call it. He swept the area one final time to make sure nothing was left behind.

"Terry just texted," Oz said to me, while Finn was in the guest room. Terry was Oz's contact in real estate. "He said for you to take some more pictures of the property and send them to him. Sounds like you'll get some heavy biters. I'll text you his email address."

Finn came around the corner. "Done," he affirmed. Then he and Oz hugged me goodbye. When Oz got into the car, Finn popped back into the house and headed toward the guest bedroom. "Sorry," he said. "I forgot my watch." I was straightening a dish towel at the sink when he returned, fastening it to his wrist. "It was good to hang out. And this is a nice place," he added, gesturing around. He stalled, and I knew he was fishing for words. "Can I ask you something?" I nodded because I recognized his tone. "This morning over breakfast, what was that all about?"

"Which part?" I replied, knowing full well what he meant. I felt the emotions swelling in my chest and up into my throat. Tears beaded under my eyes, and I hung my head, afraid to look at Finn. I knew if I did, I might fall apart right there in the kitchen. I was just tired of losing people I loved.

"Because," Finn continued. "You know you and Joanna were very happy together. You dated within a week of meeting each other, and you stayed together ever since."

Two tears puddled large enough to spill over my

cheeks, which I quickly swiped away. "I know what it's like to lose someone," Finn said, lowering his voice into that old gentle tone he used when discussing something private and sacred. "I also know from experience that if you keep this up, this reserved attitude, dwelling on your loss instead of what you still have in front of you, you'll feel this way for the rest of your life. If I didn't care about you, I wouldn't say anything."

Keeping my eyes averted, I nodded and cleared my throat. Death and misery were no strangers to Finn. If anyone had a right to curse and mourn over a life of loss, it was Clayton Finn Fincannon. As a toddler, he lost his parents and brother, then his grandfather passed away right after his college graduation. During grad school, he had to deal for years with Eden's disappearance. She went missing without any of the explanations one would need for closure. They were reunited, yes, but that took years. It's a long story, and one you can read about in his memoir, *The Mason Jar*.

Finn didn't have to say that loss is a part of life and that we must press on anyhow. Or that knowing we could lose our loved ones at any moment helps us treasure them and keep life in its proper perspective.

When Finn gave me a final hug goodbye, I drew a shaky breath and embraced him as a brother. "Call us if you need us," he said. Then they left. I watched from the kitchen window until the tail lights grew smaller and vanished around the road's bend. The only thing better than a friend who lets you be yourself is a friend who will also tell you the truth.

I thought about Finn's words, how he said to dwell on the beauties still in my life. I thought about how I owned my own condo at Pepperdine. I now owned a vineyard and the little cottage where I had spent my childhood summers. I had a decent paying job and I had my health.

There were plenty of great facets in life for me to dwell on and be thankful for. Despite all this, I also knew that I felt lonely and discouraged. Now, with my friends gone and me being alone in my deceased grandmother's home, all I really wanted to do was curl up in a ball on the bed and cry.

Chapter 10

The afternoon wore on once my friends left. To get out of my head, I went for a walk along the countryside, exploring dirt paths and four-wheeler trails that weren't there when I was a boy. I could smell the dandelions, and I could see their seeds floating through the air like snowflakes. Soon I found solace in the green wilderness around me and the songs of birds whose names I had forgotten.

I found the old creek and followed the current to where it emptied into the indigo-blue hole. Everything still looked the same, except that the old willow tree and rope swing were gone. I wondered if a storm had knocked them down. I walked up to the old giant oak that overlooked the vineyard, just a stone's throw away from the bordering woods.

A blue jay landed in the tree's branches, joining red birds, blue birds, and yellow hammers that city folk call yellow birds. More birds filled the sugar maples along the woods' edge. I lay down under it and looked up through the limbs. The boy I once was used to lie in that exact spot and dream about all the distant countries he'd explore one day.

I don't know how long I was out, but the chill in the air woke me. I had fallen asleep and the sun had already set. I felt a hunger coming on. Since I was leaving the next morning, I knew there was no sense in going to the grocery store. I remembered a cheese shop that used to be in Arrington and wondered if it was still there, so I drove into town and found a strip mall which now included a women's boutique, a coffee shop in place of the cheese shop, and a little Italian restaurant called Edison's. Through the windows, candlelight reflected off every oak table.

Cars were parked out front, along the side, and in the back. I found a spot along the curb. In the street, you could already smell fresh basil and baguette baked in open-fire ovens.

Edison's was built with glass walls and heavy doors, and it had dark-stained oak wooden floors and matching chairs with black cushions. The servers were well-groomed and wore starched white dress shirts, black slacks, and matching aprons. Candle holders the size of fists sat on every table with all their candles lit. The vibe was quiet and sophisticated.

Those dining wore dinner jackets and dresses. Behind an oak podium stood the hostess, a tall blonde with her hair pulled back and a model's posture. She wore gaudy glasses and smiled through her bright red lipstick. Only two tables were available, so she led me to one beside a window.

Joanna would have loved this place, I thought.

"I can start you off with a drink," said the hostess. She handed me a food menu and a wine list with selections from California, Oregon, and Washington. At the top of the list: Franklin Vineyard's reds and whites.

"I'll take an iced tea," I replied. I wasn't in the mood to taste any wines. I liked an occasional Pinot in Malibu. After a weekend of thinking too much about the vineyard, I didn't feel much like drinking.

As I perused the menu, examining the various lasagnas, a waitress walked into my peripheral vision, holding two bowls. When I glanced up and into her eyes, I saw that it was Rachel. "What are you doing here?" I exclaimed. It came out like a knee-jerk question. I was surprised and smitten by her beauty all at once. Her hair was pinned up again in her usual messy knot, and a few strands of her hair were matted to her glistening forehead. In her eyes, I saw exhaustion and slight annoyance at finding me sitting before her. I was left gaping at her.

"I'm the manager," she replied sharply. "I've been here ten years. It's like home. You can leave, you know," she added, this time quiet and controlled.

"I thought–"

"What, that I spend all my time at the vineyard? Dad told you I worked as a waitress. Weren't you listening?"

Apparently Rachel didn't speak sharply to guests often, because two of the servers nearby had stopped what they were doing to watch us. One stared at me with an alarmed expression.

Rachel turned and strode to a couple awaiting their tomato soup. A spirit of professionalism washed over her, like a skilled actress changing into character as she walked onto the stage. She gently sat the two bowls in front of the couple and offered a shining smile.

Seeing her in her managerial role, both serving and directing, I understood how she won people's respect. She worked hard at the vineyard, at the shop, and also at Edison's. She looked professional, and tired, and so lovely all at once. "What have I gotten myself into?" I mused. I didn't believe anything would ever happen between us, but I also knew that I'd never forget her.

Rachel had moved on, working the room. And I sat there, wondering if it was best that I leave, in case my presence would hinder her from her duties. Maybe it would be too awkward or embarrassing. I didn't know. The guests eating at the tables on both sides of me had heard the exchange. Their lingering stares and whispers made the restaurant feel more suffocating with every passing second, so I stood and quietly left.

I crossed the street to my car. The caution light blinked on and off, that same caution light that had hung there when I was a boy. There were so many beautiful facets to Tennessee, but I knew it wasn't home. There was a lack of diversity in Franklin, in both ethnicity and thought, but there was beauty and innocence in the minds of people who had never left their small towns.

I had come to prefer the excitement of the bustling SoCal cities compared to the peace and serenity of the Tennessee countryside. I could see both lives: discussing new ideas over exquisite dinners in West Hollywood–or going to bed after a shower and a warm meal, surrounded by fresh air and the sounds of the woods and pastures at night.

"She looked so lovely," I said to myself as Rachel's image ran through my thoughts. "She works so hard, and she's so passionate, and people like me have to ruin it for her." I felt like I was playing the selfish, rich, spoiled landlord, ruining the lives of the locals in an old western movie. At any moment John Wayne or Clint Eastwood would step in and have me shot or pistol-whipped.

∽∾

Still hungry, I went back to Grandmothers, packed my bags, and changed my flight. It cost me an extra $150 and was the last flight to Los Angeles that night. I couldn't wait to get out of Franklin and away from Rachel. When I jumped in the car and headed to the airport, I passed by the Youngs' home. The lights shone through the curtains, and it looked peaceful, sitting there on the edge of Grandmother's vineyard.

I felt solid guilt for the first time. Sure, there had been hints of it before, but now, the twisting was growing into plain ol' gut wrenching. The Youngs were good, hard-working people. Grandmother loved them and they loved her. I kept driving anyway, heading to the airport and away from those problems.

I kept envisioning Rachel behind the counter at the wine shop when I saw her for the first time, then under the trellis, and then at Edison's. I was probably ten minutes from the airport and twenty minutes from the vineyard when a *POW!* came from under the hood. The power steering went out. The car had thrown the belt which turned the alternator and kept the engine cool.

The car rental company was already closed for the night, so to keep from ruining the transmission, I turned around. I blasted the heater to help keep the motor cool while I drove back to the cottage.

I called a taxi service, but they were all based in Nashville, and by the time a taxi would reach Franklin, I wouldn't make my flight. Tired and frustrated, feeling the loss of so many things, including the respect of the Youngs, I did the only thing I knew to do. I drank a glass of milk to coat the hunger in my stomach, and I went to bed.

When I woke the next morning, I found that I had fallen asleep in my clothes and on top of the covers. My shoes were lying on the floor. I vaguely remembered pushing them off.

I cooked my eggs over-easy and downed them with a glass of orange juice, while talking and being put on hold by the rental car company. They said they'd deliver another vehicle in a few hours. They refunded my money and gave me two free weeks. The airline wasn't as accommodating. After they confirmed with the car rental about the malfunction, they weren't able to book another flight for three more days. I probably could have chosen a different airline, but that would mean wasting a free flight, so I decided to just stick it out in Tennessee for the weekend. My flight would leave Tuesday afternoon.

I dumped my clothes into the washing machine. I rummaged through Grandmother's closet, pulling out all the men's clothing. I found some nice shirts, though the collars were too wide for today's fashion, but they'd suffice until Tuesday. Also, in a stack in the back, there were some old jeans and t-shirts. The t-shirts were a size too large, and the jeans were too loose in the waist, but a belt would hold them up.

In the utility room, beside the washer and dryer, I found a sunhat, garden gloves, and a pair of rubber work boots half a size too large. If double-socked, provided I didn't do a lot of walking, they could be useful.

I remembered Grandmother's Gator in the shed. I felt certain it needed to be taken for a spin. I shut my eyes and turned my face away from the dust as I threw the tarp off. I cranked it, and off I went. I rode through the little backroads, passing by various farm homes and pastures. I saw stone fences here and there, barns on the hillsides, and children playing on swing sets and trampolines. I watched the horses graze and a colt bucking and swinging its head as if to remove something from its nose.

I thought of exploring Leiper's Fork, but as I passed by the Youngs' home, I spotted Michael driving a tractor with a front-end loader. He emptied a load of trash onto a pile of brush and scrap metal where their driveway met the main road. The city would pick it up within days.

Michael was preparing the property for the fall festival.

Hired hands wore straw hats and long-sleeved cotton shirts for protection against the sun. They trimmed vines here and there, but mostly pulled weeds from around the end posts and beneath the dangling green grapes. I went back and grabbed the sun hat and leather gloves from Grandmother's utility room and rode the Gator to Michael's barn.

I walked over to him while sliding on the gloves. Evelyn was straightening and sweeping the porch, and she stopped to watch. Knowing I was supposed to fly out that day, they probably wondered why I was still there. When Michael saw me approaching, he dropped the throttle to dull the tractor's roar. "I thought I'd give you a hand," I yelled over the engine's rattle. "A belt came off the car, so I'm stuck until Tuesday."

"You still selling the place?" Michael asked.

"Yes, sir," I replied.

Michael nodded and looked away. He wasn't going to get upset or complain about it anymore. I think he had come to accept it and would make do with what came their way. "While I'm here," I offered, "I can help you get this place in shape for the festival. I don't have anything else to do."

Michael gazed across the vineyard at Evelyn, who still watched us. "Fair enough," he said. "If you want to help, I'll pull the tractor around and you can help me load all the junk. You'll have to use a shovel because the grass grew up around some of it. It's old stuff from the fermenting. We don't use it anymore."

Michael raised the gas throttle on the tractor, the engine stuttered louder, and he and I worked together. We piled the shed's remains onto the front-end loader, chopped down the overgrowth with a sling blade, and dug up thistle roots.

From inside the house, Rachel stepped out, carrying a basket of cheeses for the shop. She passed by Evelyn, who was watering flowers in baskets hanging from the porch ceiling. When Rachel saw me and her dad working side by side, she looked at her mother for clues, and though Evelyn offered a smile, Rachel didn't soften at the sight of us. She just pressed on toward the shop, not looking back.

I uncovered a sun-bleached football, half-flat, in a patch of weeds beneath a tarp protecting an old plow motor. I remembered how Grandmother and I once stood near that spot years ago and tossed that same football back and forth.

Grandmother had worn stonewashed jeans and I had been wearing gym shorts so short that kids today would make fun of them. I ran out for a pass and Grandmother launched it underhanded, but it flew over my head. She slapped a knee and laughed as I ran after it.

I held the football in the air for Michael to see. When he clapped his hands, I tossed it to him. Michael hopped off the tractor, and I went out for a long one. Michael launched it, and this time I caught it, and faked a touchdown by dancing in an invisible end zone. Michael gave a thumbs-up. I don't believe he had thrown a football in years. Neither had I.

When the work and play was done, we sat in chairs under the trellis, with the early evening sun behind us. Evelyn brought us glasses of iced tea and chicken salad sandwiches mixed with diced walnuts, celery, and sliced grapes.

After the lawn care crew arrived to mow and weed-whack the property, Michael said in passing that he was finished outside, so I took that as my cue to leave. We shook hands, he thanked me for my help, and I returned to Grandmother's house.

∞

The rental car company was delivering the SUV when I arrived back at the cottage. I thanked them, looked the SUV over for dings and scratches, and signed the release forms. As soon as they left, I took a shower. It felt amazing when I stepped out. My body ached in a good way and in all the right places. Other than mowing grass, I couldn't remember the last time I worked in a yard.

Feeling refreshed, I bounced from the bedroom to the kitchen wearing clean clothes, thanks to Grandmother's collection. I looked myself over in the bathroom mirror. I wore jeans with a belt, and a v-neck t-shirt with a button down dress shirt on top, which fit just fine.

In the kitchen, I opened the fridge… to nothing. A little milk and some iced coffee Finn left, and a bowl of biscuits from two days before. There was still time to go into Franklin and stock up on two days' worth of groceries, but I didn't want to go there yet. In the pantry I found that jar of local honey, so I splattered some onto the biscuits.

I grabbed some iced coffee and took it with the biscuits onto the back porch to view the pastures and vineyard. The air felt nice. Horses swished their tails, lazily. Lightning bugs pulsed and dipped in the sky, and I was serenaded by the songs of tree frogs, cicadas, and katydids. The scent of fresh cut grass lingered in the air, and I could feel the beginnings of the coming dew.

"Hey!" came Grandmother's voice. I turned around, and there she was. I was thirteen again, standing in that same place, with my hands in my pockets. The sun had already set and twilight had turned to dusk. "What are you thinking about?" she asked.

"It's peaceful out there," I replied, turning my eyes back to the wonders and mysteries of the countryside at night.

"Not like the city, is it?" she asked, sauntering over to join me. I shook my head. "And you thought I lived out here because I'm an old woman. Well, you're right," she said, looking out at the open fields by my side.

"What's out there, at night?"

"Well, insects you don't see during the day. Owls, foxes. I don't know. Possums."

"Anything else?"

"Well, if you want me to be a philosopher, I could say that what's out there is what you take with you. In here." And she pointed to her heart.

"Do you miss the city?" I asked, after a moment.

"When you're young," she said, "the city's alive and exciting. But when you're older, the countryside's that way. Always have a place to get away to, Ryan. It will help you find peace."

I woke from my daydream, downed the last of my coffee, and stepped back into the cottage. Lonely, and never one to watch TV, I couldn't decide what to do. Grocery shopping sounded boring. I couldn't visit Michael. We were getting along much better, but Michael was tired. Besides, I knew not to overstay my welcome.

My mind wandered to Rachel. I thought of her smile, which showed all her teeth when she laughed really hard. I thought of how her family and colleagues liked and respected her, how if we had met under different circumstances, we might have gotten along well–maybe even dated.

Oz and Finn approved of her. I could even say they probably hoped she and I would hit it off. I knew I didn't have anything to lose by talking to her again. She already disliked me, so I was at rock bottom with her anyway. The only direction we could go was up.

I knew from experience that when it comes to dating and marriage, asking, "Am I good enough for her, or is she good enough for me?" misses the mark. It's better to ask, "Are we a good fit, or are we compatible?" If you truly want to get to know someone, you just have to spend long periods of time together in a variety of circumstances. Family and friends will have their opinions of who you date, but quality time spent together is the only sure way to uncover someone's true character.

So I hopped into my new SUV, cranked it up, and headed to Edison's to see Rachel.

Chapter 11

When I arrived, there was a line at the door. Guests stood with their arms crossed, and one or two rolled their eyes and muttered complaints. Others sat on park benches and played on their phones. Inside, people lined the walls. Servers rushed plates to tables, refilled drinks, filled orders. Even the hostess was helping deliver plates. Apparently, a conference had taken place in Nashville and a tour bus stopped for dinner on its way back to Alabama.

Rachel sped from the kitchen to the hostess, scanned the seating charts, and calmed those who threatened to leave. I heard a tray of plates crash in the kitchen, and that's when I stepped forth. "You have a packed house," I said to Rachel as she whizzed by.

When she saw me, her face didn't change at all. "I don't have time to waste with you," she pointed out, icily. A waitress tapped her on the shoulder, asked a question, and Rachel pointed toward the back corner of the restaurant.

"Where're all your servers?" I persisted, ignoring her clear dislike of me.

"Why do you care?" she shot back. "There's restaurants in downtown Franklin who'll be glad to take your money."

Another guest raised his hand, complaining over another wrong order, so Rachel rushed to help, then she jetted through a swinging door into the kitchen. On her way back out, her arms were filled with plates. Behind her, in the heat of the kitchen's flames, yells blared from the only chef on duty.

After Rachel passed off a plate to the hostess, she caught a glimpse of me wearing an apron and scribbling down people's orders. My pizzeria days back in Calgary paid off. The vibe and tempo of the two restaurants weren't that different. With a tweak or two, thanks to some pointers from other servers, I caught on pretty quick.

"What are you doing?" Rachel blurted, marching over to me. She didn't seem offended. It was more of a knee-jerk reaction.

"I was a waiter in college," I explained. "One of the finest hole-in-the-wall restaurants in town." I meant it as a joke, but Rachel wasn't smiling.

"I don't care," she snorted.

I purposefully scanned the room and all its chaos, then turned back to Rachel. At that exact moment, another set of dishes crashed in the kitchen.

"Fine," she conceded, slapping her hips in surrender. "Just fill everyone's glasses." She gestured to the pitcher stand.

I had already taken one table's order, so I ripped off the paper and handed it to the waitress passing behind us. She glanced at it, nodded at Rachel, and carried on. After I filled everyone's drinks, I pressed onto the next customers to take orders. I glanced over my shoulder at Rachel, and she was watching me with an expression of surprise. I guessed she could tolerate me for an evening.

The night passed quickly. Drinks and orders were delivered, customers were satisfied, and people trickled in then out again, once their stomachs were filled. After the rush hours ended, I caught Rachel watching me every now and then. Relief had washed over her face. She also wore a smile, making me wonder if she was a bit impressed by me. I liked to think so, at least.

By 9 p.m. Edison's was half-empty, and Rachel strode up to me. She put her hands on her hips and exhaled a tired breath, blowing the hair out of her eyes. "I think we're good," she announced. "Thanks for your help." I knew she meant it was time for me to leave, but I wanted to stay and see how this played out. Rachel, not knowing what else to say, swept her hands to the door, an obvious request for me to go.

"You're welcome," I replied with a smile. In the back, one of the servers I had helped motioned me to the kitchen window. There sat one last plate for a guest I'd been serving. I pushed past Rachel and delivered it promptly. "You were saying?" I asked her when I returned. She bit back a flustered smile.

"I was wondering," she answered, as she lifted two

dirty plates. She nudged her head toward the kitchen for me to follow her. "How can a guy who seems so helpful, like yourself, be so selfish?"

"You don't know me," I replied, chuckling.

"I think I've seen quite a bit," she confirmed.

"Do you always talk down to your volunteers?" I asked, with a cocked brow.

"No one volunteers," she argued. "They always get something in return, even if it's just to feel good." She slid the plates onto the windowsill and turned to face me. "But no one I know is as puzzling to me, either. It's like you're a different person every time I meet you." She tilted her head to the side. "Do you have a split personality?"

"The only way you'll get to know me is by spending time with me," I answered.

"That will never happen," she stated with a final nod.

A remaining guest raised his hand and Rachel went to see him. He asked for a to-go box. I didn't want to stand there like a dummy, so I refilled some drinks at a nearby table. When Rachel passed behind me, she added, "I'd never spend time with anyone who makes the kind of remarks about love that you do."

"Why, because I'm guarded?"

"No, because you're arrogant. That little professor tone you use. You're looking down at divorcees while you're divorced, too."

"I don't look down at divorcees," I retorted. I didn't realize, until that moment, how deep my words affected her, and I decided from that moment on that I wouldn't hold back with who I was. I would treat her with care and humility.

"It's like you're bipolar," she went on. "Did your mom drop you on your head when you were a kid or something?"

"Before she and Dad died?" I replied, as if talking about something trivial. "Probably not." Rachel recoiled at that. I didn't want to jab her, but after that last remark, it was hard not to.

What I really wanted to say was that I thought her family were good, hard-working people. And that she was pretty. And that my heart was opening to a woman again for the first time since Joanna. But I couldn't, unless I wanted to scare her off. Though our conversation was heated, it was a step in the right direction. She needed to vent, and so did I. Though I wished things could've been different between us, and I hadn't put my foot in my mouth, she reminded me of a fear I had long forgotten: that I might finally open myself up, only to have my heart ripped out again.

"Look," I said, my voice softening. "I shouldn't have said what I did that first night we met, or any of the other comments I made about relationships over breakfast the next day, but I was in pain." I closed the notepad I was carrying and tapped it against my hand. Then I took a step closer to her, so close I could have taken her in my arms. "Joanna and I didn't divorce. She died in childbirth." Rachel pulled her head back to examine my face, and by her expression, I knew she believed me.

"Just so you know," I added, knowing I needed to say

one more thing before leaving. "After all that's happened, I like your family. They're good people." Rachel looked away, her eyes glazing over. Her lip quivered when she looked back up at me. She was about to cry, which wasn't the reaction I had expected or intended to bring about in her. I saw one of the servers slowing in her step, keeping her eye on us, so I handed Rachel the notepad, and walked out the door.

Chapter 12

The next morning, a Monday, I took photos of the vineyard for the real estate agent. I was leaving the next day, and it was time to place the property on the market. I took wide shots of the countryside, then of Grandmother's house, and even shot artsy angles of all the windows and doors. I zoomed in on a picnic basket with grapes pouring out, with a blurry door as the backdrop. I took photos of the side of the cottage, with the dogwoods and redbuds framing the window.

It was lunchtime when I finished. I wasn't too hungry, so I sliced some apples and dipped them in a jar of caramel I fished out of the pantry. I sat with my laptop at Grandmother's desk, transferred the photos, typed in the real estate agent's email, and pressed send. I leaned back in the chair and stared out the window. I kept seeing Rachel in my mind, but pushed her away. To distract myself, I opened the top desk drawers to see what Grandmother had left lying around. I found a stack of white paper, thick and coarse with the Franklin

Vineyard letterhead imprinted on the upper left corner of every page. It took me back to memories of Grandmother sitting at her desk, writing fancy letters to friends. A glass of Cabernet sat near her hand.

I was a kid again, lying on her bed, throwing the football into the air and catching it. I was bored, waiting for her to finish her adult duties. She said she'd toss the ball with me later and, to me, later felt like an eternity.

"Never underestimate the power of writing letters," she said with her back to me. "Professionals love handwritten letters in a time when everybody uses typewriters."

"But that's good, right?" I reasoned aloud. "For people to think you have a typewriter? It means you're successful." Back then, typewriters were as expensive as computers are today.

"Typewriters have their purpose," she answered. "But nothing beats the care of a handwritten letter."

A knock came at the front door, interrupting my daydream. When I peeked through the window, I saw Michael. He stood with his hair perfectly slicked back, as usual. His face was unshaven and he wore a button-down dress shirt, untucked, over khakis. His smile was warm, and he waved hello. "Hi Michael," I said as I opened the front door. "You want to come in?"

"No, thanks," he answered. "Just letting you know, we're having supper at our house tonight. We'd like you to join us."

"I'd be honored," I replied, surprised at the invitation. I wondered if he and Evelyn heard that I had helped at the restaurant, or perhaps it was a small thank you for helping with the manual labor. Or maybe they were just kind, hospitable people.

"Can I bring something?" I asked.

"Nope, just yourself." Then he waved goodbye. "4:30," he called behind him mid-stride.

I took a shower, brushed my teeth, and combed my hair. I fingered through the shirts hanging in Grandmother's closet. The pickings were slim, but I selected a shirt and rolled up the sleeves. I slipped on some khakis, fashionable enough.

I drove to a local mom-and-pop market on the outskirts of Franklin and bought some assorted flowers. Michael implied they didn't need food, but I didn't want to show up empty-handed. As I pulled up into the Youngs' driveway, Oz called.

"Terry said the photos you took were great," Oz said. "He's already had three people wanting vineyards, and they don't even care if the wine's good."

"Great! Nice work."

"Yeah, and get this. He thinks he can get you at least a million."

"A million? Wow." That was terrific because I could pay off my student loans, have my professor's pension, and then add to that, the funds from the estate. I'd be able to live comfortably in retirement.

"You're sitting on a gold mine, bro," Oz said, just as Michael came to the door and waved me in. I told Oz I needed to go, thanked him again, and hung up.

When I stepped inside the Youngs' home, the smell of roasted lamb and garlic permeated the air, making my stomach growl.

Evelyn wore a red apron over a yellow summer dress, and was placing a glass bowl of brown rice on the table. She went to the sink to wash a head of lettuce. On the dining room table sat various platters of food: Sweet potato casserole, green beans, turnip root, and cream cheese stuffed jalapeños wrapped in bacon. Two candles in tiny square glass holders softened the light in the room.

"Hi Dr. Lockwood," Evelyn said, smiling.

"Hi, Evelyn. You can call me Ryan," I replied, presenting the flowers.

"Thank you. They're lovely. Just lay them on the counter. I'll find a vase."

"I'll get some wine," Michael said, and disappeared into a back room. Evelyn lay the head of lettuce on a cutting board and flicked the water off her fingers. She took a vase from the top of the refrigerator, filled it half-full with water, and set the flowers in it. Then she placed them at the center of the table.

Julie and her fiancé Charlie came from her bedroom and shook my hand. Charlie had red wavy hair, a slim physique, and bright blue eyes. His face held no blemishes, and he seemed to always be smiling.

He was a year younger than Julie, grew up knowing her, and had always been in love with her, but never told her. He was working in the healthcare industry in Houston, Texas when Julie divorced and moved home. When Charlie heard about it, he quit his job, returned to Franklin, and they had been dating ever since. As Grandmother used to say, "Just because something is meant to be, doesn't mean it's meant to be right now."

Julie held a glass of red wine in her hand, and Charlie was sipping bourbon over ice. "Rachel's working tonight," Julie said. "I'm sorry." I wondered if she was testing me, because she kept her eyes on me, without blinking, as if she was watching for a reaction.

I shrugged, like the news was commonplace. "Well, she probably doesn't want to see me anyway," I replied. "I'd spoil her dinner."

Julie laughed and patted my arm. "No, you wouldn't," she said. I could tell she sincerely meant it, and that's all I needed to know. Sisters talk, and if that was Julie's reaction, I hoped that Rachel had said something redemptive about me. When Julie noticed her mother chopping lettuce, she stepped away to help.

"Julie said you teach literature," Charlie said.

"Yeah," I acknowledged. "Yourself?"

"I'm in healthcare." Charlie had one hand in his pocket while the other held his bourbon. His shoulders were relaxed.

"Oh, that's great," I went on. "A booming industry in Nashville, I hear."

"It is," Charlie answered, smiling with a nod.

Evelyn announced supper was ready, and we gathered around the lamb while Michael raised his glass to toast.

"It's nice to sit around a table after a good day's work," he proclaimed. "And to have Sandra's grandson join us."

"Thank you," I answered as we all brought our glasses together. "It's an honor." And when I said it, Michael smiled at me.

Mashed potatoes, spinach, and squash encircled the lamb. Warm sourdough rolls baked from scratch laid in a bowl covered by a hand towel. In the middle of the table sat pitchers of iced tea and sangria, and three bottles of red wine without labels.

I wondered how many years they had sat in Michael's basement, and more importantly, what each of them tasted like. I assumed they were from the vines he managed. He poured the wine. It tasted like a dark, rich cherry with a light hint of coffee, a bit cool from having sat in the cellar. I liked it. Sure, it was nothing like a good Pinotage from California or South Africa, but it wasn't bad for Tennessee.

"So, everything's going well?" Michael asked me, as we sat and the food was passed around.

"Yes, sir."

"Sandra's cottage okay?" he added, and I nodded.

Evelyn looked at me and pointed to the lamb. "That was butchered on my brother's farm this week. Still fresh."

"Looks great," I replied.

The front door opened, and we all jerked our heads around, and it was Rachel.

Chapter 13

Rachel wore her white dress shirt untucked, and it was stained with splattered soups and sauces. Her step was sluggish, and her hair was a mess–but an endearing mess. Her eyes met mine, and though she stubbed her toe, she recovered quickly.

By her expression, I could see she had no idea I would be there. I glanced at Julie who dropped her eyes and pressed her lips together to keep from smiling. She had seen the reactions on both our faces.

"There she is!" "How was work?" "Grab some food!" everyone exclaimed, but I just sat quietly and watched her. "Hi everyone," she answered. "No, thank you. I already ate."

She walked around the table, hugging and kissing her loved ones, which they gladly received. I was on the opposite side, so when she reached me, I stood out of my chair a little and offered my hand to shake. I didn't want her to feel like she had to treat me with the same kind of affection. She nodded and gave a small chuckle when our hands met. She hadn't seen that gesture coming, but I reasoned she knew why I did it, and that I was being considerate. "You look nice," I said, lowering my voice.

Her eyes lingered on mine a moment, and I think she wondered if I was mocking her. But I wasn't, and when she suddenly realized that, she said, "Thanks. I wish." Her face flushed pink as her eyes left mine and scanned the faces of her family. "I'll have a shower and then some wine," she added, as she made her way to her bedroom.

Just as she turned the corner, she glanced over her shoulder at me. It wasn't a look of disgust or annoyance, but like someone examining me from a distance after being introduced for the first time.

"When you come out, you should play for us!" Michael called, but Rachel had already shut her door.

"She's really good," Charlie said to me.

"The piano?"

"The guitar," he answered. That was news to me. I knew her mother played the piano, but hadn't heard that her daughters were musically inclined.

"I'll get the chocolate pie," Evelyn announced, standing. Charlie told me that Evelyn made her pie from cocoa beans shipped in from the side of a mountain in Liberia. Michael knew the distributor.

After more wine was passed around, the jokes came more easily, and so did the laughs. All of Evelyn's pie was eaten, except a piece saved for Rachel. As the third bottle was uncorked, Rachel's bedroom door opened, and she came out in a white linen shirt loosely tucked into jeans, and her wet, dark hair thrown up into a French bun. She had applied a little eyeliner and light lipstick, which brought forth her natural beauty. "She did that on purpose," I thought. "How can a woman do so little and look so amazing?"

When I glanced back at the family, Julie was watching me. I knew she caught me gaping at Rachel, and a small smile bloomed on her lips as she looked back at Charlie. Julie was entertained by me.

I felt a sensation I hadn't felt in years. It was a pulsing in my throat. The last time I felt that pulse was back in college with Joanna.

Evelyn handed Rachel a glass of wine, and Michael pointed to the guitar. It stood partially hidden on the other side of the piano, beside a bar stool. "Play for us," Michael said. Rachel looked at Julie as if to say, "Save me!" But Julie only nodded in agreement. From what I understood, Rachel had only played for family. Certainly not in front of strangers, but did she think of me as a stranger? Maybe not anymore.

Rachel took a sip from her wine and set the glass on the piano. "Mom," she said, gesturing Evelyn to the piano. Rachel slid the guitar strap over her shoulder and sat on the bar stool, while Evelyn rose to join her. Rachel strummed the strings. "All I Want" by Emma Bale was the song she chose.

The lyrics tell the story of a woman whose lover has left her. She sings that when he said goodbye, a part of her died inside. But instead of succumbing to a life of bitterness, she hopes she'll find love again. The song is solemn and slow and melancholy.

I fought back tears as she sang it, not just because of the words, but because of the haunting tone. I even sipped my wine to keep the tears at bay. I didn't want anyone to see how it affected me. I wondered what the song meant privately to Rachel. Perhaps it was her own song of love and loss.

When she finished playing, everyone clapped. She smiled at their applause, and I wondered if her smile masked a thousand bittersweet memories.

The room fell quieter than before as Rachel strummed some light chords. Michael wasn't happy to hear the music end. He hopped over to the CD player and turned on The Eagles. He took Evelyn's hand and led her to the middle of the living room, and they slow danced to "I Can't Tell You Why."

Charlie and Julie fired up the espresso machine for cappuccinos, while I walked over to Rachel, holding my glass of wine. Her head was low as she focused on the strings. When she saw my feet approaching, her fingers missed a mark and a short breath escaped her. "Are you trying to surprise me again, Ryan?"

I liked the way Rachel said my name. She'd never said it before. She had always called me "Dr. Lockwood."

"I can't really see myself surprising you with anything," I answered. "Other than when I became a waiter." She chuckled at that. "You're the one who surprised me," I added.

"How so?"

"With your music."

"In a good way?" she asked, and I heard a tease in

her tone. I nodded, and then let the silence fall between us. I knew that if she wanted to talk, she'd keep the conversation going, and if she didn't, I could walk away. Just as my foot moved to leave, she spoke up. "When you first came here, you weren't smiling much. Lately, I've seen you smile a lot. Why?"

"Well, I'm feeling more comfortable here," I disclosed. Franklin was feeling more and more like home, though I couldn't bring myself to fully admit it. "I spent my summers here. And being back, it's helped."

"Be careful," she warned, grinning at me. "When my sister and I came back, we never left again, and it wasn't because we couldn't."

"I know that. And I know Grandmother stayed here for a reason. It's a good place, but my life isn't here. I belong at Pepperdine. I don't get to choose."

"Yes, you do." She paused, then added: "Your life is where you decide to build it." She looked down to tinker with her guitar strings. Not knowing what else to say, I glanced back at the party.

Michael and Evelyn were still dancing and I heard Charlie say about how good the espresso was. Julie was smiling at me and biting her lip. Now that she'd had a bit more wine, she wasn't ashamed to let me know she enjoyed watching Rachel and me. Sometimes, sisters know everything.

I wasn't smiling. I felt as if my insides were being pulled and twisted.

Chapter 14

The next morning I woke to warm beams of sunlight pouring onto the floor beside the nightstand. I had left the windows open the night before. The birds were singing and a soft breeze curled the curtains.

Thoughts of Rachel came to my mind again, but this time I didn't push them away. I thought of her stumbling through the door when she glimpsed me, laughing with guests at Edison's, singing and strumming the guitar. I thought of the soft tone in her voice now when she spoke to me.

I stepped out of bed and walked over to the window. I thought of going for another walk in the woods, maybe back to the creek where the old rope swing hung. I remembered Grandmother watching me swim. My ten-year-old self stood on the bank, holding the rope swing between my knees, dressed in nothing but swimming trunks.

"Go for it!" Grandmother shouted.

"Count down for me!" I yelled.

"Three! Two! One!"

"Geronimo!" I swung and let go, making a giant splash as I landed in the water. Grandmother laughed and cheered.

The alarm beeped on my phone, which meant my flight was due to leave in three hours. I grabbed a quick shower and repacked some last items into my suitcase. I left the kitchen counters spotless, my mattresses stripped and the sheets piled on the floor beside the washing machine.

As I was loading my suitcase into the backseat of the SUV, Michael pulled up in his old Ford truck. After he parked, he faced me with his hands in his pockets.

"Were you going to say goodbye?" he asked.

"Yeah," I answered, nodding. That was another half-truth. I planned to tell Michael goodbye over the phone, once I was at the airport.

"Did you find a buyer?"

"Lots of them."

"Wow," Michael said, looking away. "Already." He nodded thoughtfully, and after a moment, he stuck his hand out for a final handshake.

"Good luck to you, Ryan."

"You too," I answered, shaking his hand.

Michael walked back to his truck, his eyes sweeping across the property, as if he knew his time there might be limited. I felt sorry for him, but I believed things would turn out just fine. He might even grow to enjoy the new owners even more than Grandmother.

As I pulled out of the driveway, I stared out the

window across the vineyard, pastures, and hills. After living for so long on the coast in California, I realized I had missed the four seasons. SoCal's weather was always predictable, and that had its upsides, but I loved variety in Tennessee's weather. The springs were crisp, and the summers were warm with all the different shades of green. Autumn leaves boasted their glorious colors. In the winter, the countryside was powdered white, people lit fires and smoke puffed out of chimneys, and everyone got cozy over bourbons, wines, and coffee.

I could imagine living with those seasons again, but the sacrifice of my life as I knew it would be too much.

Back at Pepperdine, the sun shimmered white across the crystal blue waters. The light made the coral-colored buildings on campus glow. Students swarmed the café and sidewalks, excited to reconnect with friends and classmates and to welcome the new semester.

In the Applebee Center, home of the literature department, I knocked on the door to Dr. Willis's office. Through the door window I could see him in his chair, dressed in his dark gray suit and yellow tie. Even though he was on the phone, he motioned me in.

His glasses perched on the tip of his nose. Shelves filled with books lined three walls, and two leather chairs faced his desk. "How was Tennessee?" he asked when he hung up the phone.

"It was good," I responded, easing into one of his

soft, leather chairs.

"You're glad to be back?"

"Yes, sir."

"You got your grades loaded?" he asked, and I nodded yes. "Good." He shook his computer mouse to wake the screen. "Ready to be Chair?" I nodded again, this time with a smile. He went on. "I'll be retiring next year and I talked to Dean Davis. You're in."

"Thank you," I said, appreciatively.

"Next January, we'll start the process. Until then, let's set you up with some classes. I think you'll like what we're doing this year."

My dream had just come true, but I wasn't as excited as I imagined I'd be, not after Tennessee and meeting the Youngs. My shoulders relaxed and I nibbled the inside of my mouth, pondering. A part of me wished I had never visited the vineyard because I was already missing it.

During my first day back, Pepperdine and Malibu looked the same and smelled the same, but something was amiss. What was wrong with me? Everywhere I went, something or somewhere had always reminded me of my friends and Joanna, and I had always believed that was a good thing. But I wasn't sure about that anymore. What had changed? Life in Tennessee dominated my thoughts, and the strongest thoughts of all were about Rachel.

After Joanna passed away, I had tried to date again, but it didn't feel right. One was a young woman I had met at the coffee shop in Malibu. Another had been a former student of mine who had graduated, moved to

Calabasas, and reached out to me. Both relationships ran their short course, and I was still on good terms with both of them.

Before meeting Rachel, I liked the memories of those two women, but after Tennessee, I almost regretted dating both. The hole I thought those women could fill, I realized, was only an illusion.

Before meeting Rachel, I liked the memories of

I unpacked from the trip and restocked my fridge with groceries. When I opened the cabinet beneath the sink to empty the garbage can, I saw the vase that once sat on the dining room table. Joanna used to pick buttercups that bloomed behind our back deck, and fill the vase with them.

Later, when I went to hang up my clothes, I saw hers. I had refused to get rid of them because some still carried Joanna's scent. She loved those scarves, sweaters, jeans and dresses, and I couldn't bear to part with them.

Not long after she passed, one or two friends suggested I move out of that condo, but Joanna and I had bought it together, and that meant the world to me. Since I was faculty and she worked as staff as a chaplain's assistant, Pepperdine had created an excellent mortgage payment plan, and our home was one for the picture books. There wasn't a better view in all of Malibu.

Joanna and I drank coffee and shared breakfast at the dining table every morning, with her hand resting on top of mine, looking out at our panoramic view of the ocean.

The hummingbirds and honeybees would chase each other among the lilies, and the air was always filled with the scent of sea salt and flowers. Sounds of the seagulls echoed in the ravine that led up to our back door, and in the evenings the swallows darted and dove in the air, their bodies and wings silhouetted against the sunsets. I couldn't remember a time in my life when I was happier.

Oz and Shannon lived down the street and would often join us in the evenings. That made all of our lives sweeter. We four would enjoy supper on our balcony and watch the sun set in hues from auburn to blues, and disappear behind the cliffs that dropped straight into the ocean.

At night, when Joanna and I were alone, sometimes we'd build a fire in the fireplace and let the scent of burning oak permeate the condo. We made love by that fire, murmuring words of affection and appreciation to each other. I would trace her skin with my fingertips while we watched the flames curl around the wood. She'd fall asleep in my arms, I'd carry her to bed, and at dawn, we'd make love again.

I made it a point to tell her I loved her every day; when we returned home from work, and even when we met each other in a room after being apart for a few hours. We'd hug and whisper, "I love you."

Joanna had painted the former office pink and had already bought a crib; she was so excited to bring our daughter into the world. One of the memories I have of Joanna is of her standing beside our daughter's bedroom window, holding a paint roller, with smudges of pink paint on her cheek and in her hair.

I had been teaching and had come home early. Joanna was wearing her cut-off jean shorts and a white v-neck t-shirt. To cover her hair, she wore a navy blue bandana with a white paisley design. My heart beat faster when I saw her. That lump rose in my throat, because she looked cute, hot, sexy, and beautiful all at once. When she saw the expression on my face, she covered her mouth and laughed.

"What is it?" she implored.

"Nothing," I answered. I leaned against the door, loosened my tie, stuffed my hands into my pockets, and just watched her. She kept looking at me with a quirky smile, waiting for an honest response.

"You just look cute," I said. I walked over to her, and she started chuckling. I kissed her forehead and then her lips, and then I pulled her into a hug that I wished could last forever. That was as far as it went. We could make love later. I mean, she was busy painting our daughter's bedroom for goodness' sake!

I went into the kitchen and poured a glass of iced tea, and looked one more time over my shoulder at her. Joanna had resumed painting, but her face blushed and she was grinning. She knew my eyes were taking in all her beauty, that I wanted her, and she relished in that. She let the feeling soothe and cover her like a warm blanket. I never forgot that moment with her.

The first year after her passing was the hardest. Oz and Finn suggested I go to counseling, and I reluctantly agreed. Dr. Cates was a friend of ours, and he was a counselor at Pepperdine. When I visited him, Dr. Cates suggested that I continue returning to the places Joanna and I loved. "While you're there, say, 'This is a place we had wonderful moments together. Where we laughed and shared good times with friends.'" He said I would feel close to her again and it would help me remember life's beauty. "Dwell on those good times and those good feelings, and it will lead to you feeling close to your loved ones."

This exercise taught me that everywhere I went could be interpreted as something good and beautiful rather than something to mourn or forget. "Celebrate her memory rather than mourn your loss," Dr. Cates advised. And I did.

Finn had written me a letter shortly after Joanna died. "The time we get to spend with our loved ones is always limited," he wrote. "It's long or it's short, but we celebrate the fact that we got to be with them and love them for a certain time, and that they loved us just as fiercely. We must dwell on that, rather than on what we no longer have."

Oz's reaction was different. He had no words of wisdom to impart. He just wanted to hang out with me, and let me know I still had a home with Shannon and him.

After Joanna's burial, there were days when I felt sure that life would become normal again. Then, months dragged on when I swung daily from a deep depression to "kinda happy" and all the feelings in between.

I had other friends, of course, but they weren't

nearby. At Pepperdine and every other place I have been in the United States, everyone lives in individual units. Americans love and embrace independence, but what we often inherit with that is loneliness. I knew the few friends I had couldn't cure me of the lonely times, and it wasn't fair to expect that from them.

Sometimes I wondered if in our loneliness, we all secretly long for a village where everyone knows our name. It made me think of the villages I visited in Africa where the windows and doors were always open, and loneliness and boredom was a foreign concept.

Over time my emotional pendulum swung back and forth daily or even hourly, but other times the melancholy lingered on for weeks. I would see couples walk hand-in-hand on campus, or at the beach. I'd catch sight of little things, such as a couple leaning into each other at a pub while eating with friends, and my heart would ache.

Every now and then, Oz would catch me watching Shannon and him, and I know he could see my sadness and envy, but he never judged me. He had lost a brother when he was young, and he knew that we not only mourn the past with our deceased loved ones, but we mourn the future with them that'll never be.

I never once felt truly happy. The kind of happy where a joke made me laugh so hard that my jaw ached. I missed the comfort of going to bed at night, content and at peace, as I had when I was a child, safe with my parents, or when Joanna rested in my arms under the moon and stars.

I missed eating with Joanna in SoCal's restaurants,

or cooking the vegetables we had selected that morning at the farmer's market. After she was gone, eating felt like a chore. Just something we humans do to stay alive.

I hated the sickness that puddled in my stomach when I remembered the good times with Joanna, the awful awareness that I'd never have those times with her and our friends again.

Now that I was back from Tennessee and standing in our condo, alone, I realized how lonely I had felt these last two years. Joanna's scent had disappeared from all her clothes. There were no sounds of the woman I loved, no laughter from friends around our dining table, no music from Joanna's iPad, which while she was alive, I'd often wished she'd leave off. "I like the noise," she would say. Actions of hers I once found annoying, I now missed dearly.

Pepperdine was once the village I called home, but when Finn and Eden left, even though Oz and Shannon remained, a lot of that village-feeling was lost, and then Joanna was gone. It wasn't until I returned from Tennessee that the reality fully began to resonate within me. Pepperdine wasn't much of a village to me anymore.

The next morning, I made a phone call to Oz, and then I made another one to Kim Satterfield. The vineyard would be taken off the market. I didn't have a plan. I just knew Grandmother's property was no longer for sale.

Chapter 15

I received a voicemail from Michael a few days later on my cell phone. He had called while I was teaching. He thanked me for not selling the vineyard, and said he would be traveling to UC Irvine in a week to pick up some vines.

Since he would be in the area, he had scheduled a meeting with Dr. Forrester in Pepperdine's horticulture department. Michael wondered if I'd be available for supper. When I called him back, he didn't answer, so I left him a message that he was most welcome here, and to just let me know when he was on his way to Malibu.

A week passed.

I had just finished class, was wearing my gray suit and white dress shirt, and had stepped into the back hallway of the Applebee Center. It's the shortest distance between the classroom and my office. I had my phone glued to my ear, talking to a rep at a gym because I was getting back into my workout regiment. My other hand held a stack of papers.

The Applebee Center is a state-of-the-art building. Once you pass through any one of the doors, the scent of fresh carpet hits your nose. Framed photos of students who won Fulbright scholarships hung on the light cream walls. The main entrance to our hall was through two glass doors with silver bars for handles. "Literature Department" was painted on them with a white sandy texture.

The office secretary's desk sat out front, with a Mac computer on top. Cushioned chairs for visitors lined the walls across from her desk. Behind her, to the left, was the office of the Chair, but down a hallway to the right, professor offices sat every ten feet apart. That's where my office was.

Ms. Becky, the office secretary, was a short, stubby woman with straight blonde hair. She wore apple-red reading glasses affixed to a black retainer rope that hung behind her neck. Ms. Becky was a kind woman, direct, and professional, like a grandmother who had been wise even in her youth and who had heard and seen it all.

I was walking and talking, and I saw her at the end of the hall. Ms. Becky had her office phone to her ear, and she was waving at me to come to her desk. She had never done that before, and given the energy and intensity of her wave, I knew it had to be important.

"A young woman just scooted out that way," she informed me, one hand covering the mouth piece and the other hand gesturing down the hall. "She was here to see you–from Tennessee."

Michael hadn't called, but that young woman could

only be one person. Rachel. I dropped my papers on Ms. Becky's desk and hurried out the front doors into the courtyard where sidewalks led like the spokes of a wheel to every other building on campus. Striding across the parking lot away from me, with her eyes focused down on her phone, was Rachel. I felt my heart hop. Her hair was pulled back into a ponytail, and she was wearing a white dress shirt tucked into new jeans.

"Rachel!" I yelled as I hurried after her, but she kept going. "Rachel!" I yelled louder, and picked up my pace. She froze, and I knew then that she had heard me both times. Sheepish, she turned around just as I was about twenty feet from her. She appeared almost afraid to look me in the eyes, like she was embarrassed. I didn't slow down until I was within arm's reach of her.

I hesitated a moment, then took two more steps and hugged her. That surprised her. I know because it took her a second longer to hug me back, but I detected sincerity in her touch.

"I wasn't expecting you," I said, when I pulled back.

"I know," she replied, a smile breaking free. "And I'm sorry. Dad said he tried to call you."

"No, it's okay. He called last week, and I returned his call, but that was it."

"He tried calling you back, but it kept going to voicemail."

"That's okay," I reassured. "Cell reception can be spotty. So he's here?"

"Yeah. He's with Dr. Forrester. I was just walking around and I saw the literature department, so I walked in. I hope that's all right."

"Sure it is," I replied, surprised that she'd think otherwise. I looked closely at her, happy to see her again. She wore pearl earrings and looked southern and lovely.

"I thought you were teaching class," she explained.

"No. I'm not. Not right now." I wasn't trying to be funny, and she didn't laugh. I think we were both too nervous.

"I came with Dad," she added. "You didn't know I was coming?"

"No."

Three seconds of white-hot silence felt like minutes.

"How was your class?" she asked, fidgeting with her hands. I had never seen her nervous in front of me before. I found it flattering and somewhat of a relief.

"It was fine," I answered. "How's the vineyard?"

"Good." Rachel brought her hands together in front of her as if to pray, then intertwined her fingers, unsure what to say next. "Thank you for what you did," she said, finally. "For not selling the property. Dad was so happy. We all were." Then, she looked away and her shoulders relaxed.

"Do you want to come in?" I asked, meaning the Applebee Center. "I have a while before my next class."

"I can't," she replied. "I have to find Dad."

"Okay. Well, I think he wanted to get supper." She nodded and I could tell she didn't know Michael meant to make supper plans. A part of me panicked, because I was afraid Michael may have changed his mind about staying longer.

"I'll tell you what," I said. "The Ag department is on the other side of this building." I pointed behind us, to where the theater stood. "I need to wrap up a few things, but I'll meet you and your dad there. Okay?"

"Sounds great," she agreed. Another smile broke free. When she walked away, she never looked back at me, but I didn't care. I felt this strange and nice sensation. I was happy to see Rachel at Pepperdine. A place I knew so well and loved.

I hurried back to the department and gathered my papers from Ms. Becky's desk. I dropped them onto my chair in my office and called Oz at the Study Abroad office.

I had an idea.

Chapter 16

About thirty minutes later, Dr. Forrester and Michael were coming out of the Ag building, looking like brothers. They both wore dress shirts tucked into worn jeans over brown carpenter work boots. The only difference was the way they combed their hair.

I saw Rachel standing on the other side of them when Oz and I approached from behind. "It's nice to see folks from Tennessee taking an interest in vine dressing," I heard Dr. Forrester say to the Youngs.

"Well, we love it," Michael remarked, laughing. "And we're interested in having your interns when everything's ready."

When Oz and I walked up, Dr. Forrester nodded hello and Michael and Rachel turned around. Michael's eyes lit up when he saw us. "Well, hey there!" he exclaimed. Rachel was smiling more easily now, and with the fond way her eyes met mine, all anxiety left me.

Everyone shook hands, and Oz even hugged Rachel, welcoming her to Pepperdine.

"Do you know these two?" Michael asked Dr. Forrester.

"Of course," he replied. "Good men. Good representatives of Pepperdine."

"I talked to my wife, Shannon," Oz said, turning to Michael. "We'd like to have you and Rachel over for dinner. You can come too, Dr. Forrester."

"Thanks," Dr. Forrester answered. "But my family has plans. It was nice having you all here," he said to the Youngs. Michael and Rachel thanked him for the tour, and Dr. Forrester waved a final goodbye and left.

"Are either of you vegetarians?" Oz asked the Youngs, keeping the conversation going.

"No," Michael said, laughing.

"No food allergies?" Oz went on with a grin.

"Nope," Michael insisted. Rachel stole a glance at me and smiled again.

"Good, because I cook the best rib eye in Malibu."

"He does," I added, rocking on my heels. I couldn't help but wonder if Rachel came to Pepperdine to see me, or if it was solely to keep her dad company. I hoped it was the former.

"Sounds great," Michael replied. We parted with handshakes and hugs, and Rachel was warm against my chest when we hugged again. I breathed in her scent, which reminded me of the honeysuckle in Tennessee, and all I felt was gratitude.

We gave Michael the address to Oz's condo because he wanted to stop at Malibu Yogurt first. Michael had heard about "Malibu Yo" from friends at UC Irvine who told him that Pamela Anderson was always there. He wanted to see if he could catch a glimpse of her.

I went home with Oz and helped him and Shannon prepare supper. The wind was blowing hard, rippling the American flags and umbrellas on all the patios. So, Shannon thought it best to host the dinner at the dining room table. We could still sit with a view. Oz and Shannon's kitchen walls were also made of glass, just like mine, and this allowed us to look out across the campus and coast.

We welcomed the Youngs into the Bailey home just a few hours before sunset, for a full spread of steak, mashed potatoes, and grilled asparagus.

Shannon's golden blonde hair accented her doe-brown eyes, and I think Michael made sure he wasn't caught staring at her. Shannon was charming, hospitable, and gorgeous. Michael told me later that her face reminded him of Pamela Anderson's face. I thought that was funny because other than her blonde hair, I didn't think Shannon resembled Pamela Anderson at all.

Oz opened a bottle of Pinotage, which Michael later said was some of the best he had ever tasted. The Baileys wanted to know more about the Youngs and the vineyard, and Michael was happy to do all the talking.

He talked about tractor issues and the deer, rabbits, and raccoons that kept eating the vine leaves. He explained why the vine dressers prune two out of three bunches of grapes, so the remaining bunch receives all the nourishment and produces a higher alcohol content. He pointed out how the best sections of the vineyard face east, and he talked about laying stones around the roots to keep them warm at night, and casting nets to ward off birds and critters.

Michael enumerated how to rid the vines of odium, the vine mildew, which is hard to kill off once it spreads. There's a lot of science to maintaining a vineyard that sells its wine across the nation, and Michael didn't mind explaining every detail.

Rachel and I watched each other a lot, but didn't say much. There was lots of laughter around the table. Oz and Shannon shared stories from their trips to Italy and Ireland. They described their road trips up the coast.

Oz pointed to the empty bottle of Pinotage on the table, which we had just finished, and said it was from a boutique vineyard in St. Helena, a small town above Napa. He described how in St. Helena, American flags hang over the streets, couples walk holding hands, and flowers pour out of the baskets on the fronts of bicycles parked outside shops.

Oz and Shannon were saving that wine for "something special," Oz said, and having the Youngs over was such an occasion. Michael and Rachel thanked the Baileys profusely.

"I'm sorry you had to put up with my husband during his stay," Shannon said, now fully relaxed in the company of her guests. She leaned against Oz's shoulder and patted his arm. Her eyes shone from love and too much wine.

"He was fine," Michael replied with a dismissive wave. "It was a pleasure to have everyone there. Mr.

Fincannon, too."

"Aw," breathed Shannon. "I wish he and Eden could be here," she added, rubbing Oz's back with her hand. Then she turned to Michael, "I tasted some of your Cabernet. Oz brought some home and it was really good."

"Not bad at all, is it?" Michael agreed. "Especially when you're competing with California. But not all of our grapes are from Tennessee. We ship in a lot from California."

There was a pause in the conversation and I could tell Oz was anxious to say something to Rachel. "Did you bring your guitar?" he asked her, smiling.

"Guilty," I said, lifting my hands in surrender. "I told them you play."

"No," Rachel replied, drawing out the syllable.

"Come on," Michael continued, nudging her. "You got a guitar?" he asked Oz and Shannon. They shook their heads no.

"I didn't bring it and I'm glad I didn't," Rachel stated.

"Ryan said you can tear it up," Oz went on, grinning.

"I think Ryan exaggerates," Rachel answered.

"I didn't exaggerate," I replied. "You're good." Rachel looked away, blushing.

"Well," Shannon said. "I would have loved to have heard you play."

"She's been playing since she was a little girl," Michael added. "We tried to get her to take it to the next level, move closer to Nashville, but she wanted to stay at the vineyard. And that was fine by us."

The sky evolved to gold and pink as the evening approached. We all helped Oz and Shannon clear the table. I leaned over and whispered something into Rachel's ear, and she smiled and nodded. "We're going to step out for a second," I announced to the group. "I'm going to show her the beach."

"Okay," Oz replied.

"Just remember, our flight leaves at nine," Michael said. Rachel and I stepped out of the sliding glass door and onto the patio. I looked over my shoulder at Oz, and he winked at me while Shannon handed Michael a glass of wine. She asked him to tell her more about the vineyards of Tennessee, which I suspected she did to distract him from us.

"Oz and Shannon are great," Rachel noted, after I slid the door shut behind us.

"They are," I agreed. She stepped over to the railing and took in the sight of the water. I watched her study the waves disappearing just before they crashed beneath the cliffs, into a blue world unseen and unknown. A gust of wind lifted her hair, and she tucked the loose strands behind her ears. When she glanced over at me, I swallowed hard. I thought she looked beautiful in the rays of sunlight.

"Would you like to go down there?" I suggested. We walked to a wooden staircase, crossed the Pacific Coast Highway, and took off our shoes at the sand. Seagulls soared and cackled back and forth to each other while a dad taught two wet-haired boys, no older than six and eight, how to throw a Frisbee. Most of the people on the beach had left since the sun was setting and the temperature was dropping.

Rachel and I left our shoes at the bottom of the stairs. She rolled her jeans to her knees and we walked along the water's edge, in the wet and packed sand. The ceaseless popping of the waves drowned out all sounds from the distant roads. With the easy sun before us and a soft breeze on our cheeks, we headed into the unknown.

Chapter 17

We hadn't been on the beach five minutes when the father and two boys loaded into a truck and left. Other than an older lady collecting seashells about one hundred yards behind us, Rachel and I were alone. "You love it here, don't you?" she asked me, already knowing the answer.

"All my best adult memories are here," I replied. "From college onward. It's where I met my best friends, and it's where I fell in love for the first time." I looked toward the horizon and Rachel watched my eyes as thousands of memories played behind them.

"It's home to you," she stated, confirming the truth.

"And Tennessee's home for you," I returned.

"We come from different worlds, don't we?"

"Yeah, but I think we understand each other's worlds," I replied. "We've both been places and seen things. We both share in the human experience." I chuckled at myself. I sounded like a professor.

"What?" she asked, tapping my arm. I felt the

affection in her touch, but I didn't let on. I stepped closer to her, matched her step, and I felt my shoulders relax.

"I was just thinking about how I sounded like… a professor."

"Well, you are a professor," Rachel said, smiling up at me.

"Yeah." I'm not sure why, but it felt strange to be objective on my own life. I stuffed my hands into my pockets and felt the wind against my chest. "How're Julie and Charlie?"

"They're good."

"Your mom?" I asked, and she nodded. "You want to hear something funny?"

"What?"

"I kinda miss it there," I confessed. Rachel smiled and I watched her feet in the sand and the curve of her calves, how the tendons rolled and flexed as she walked. I had never seen her legs before, but I liked them. They were well-toned. I felt the blood rush through my neck and chest.

She made me feel anxious and nervous. In her company, the yearning to return to the vineyard became stronger. I was generally relaxed but Rachel's presence unbalanced me. Young women didn't have that effect on me anymore, and at Pepperdine, beautiful, educated, young women from good, stable families were plentiful.

Rachel had a work ethic. She had been humbled by life. She knew the difference between the majors and minors. She liked to think and talk about intelligent things. She was dedicated to her family, and she loved them deeply.

"May I ask you a personal question?" she asked, interrupting the silence and my thoughts.

"Sure," I answered.

"Do you think you'll ever get married again, or want children?"

After Joanna passed, I had thought about those questions a thousand times, and every answer was "No," but now, I wasn't sure anymore. I couldn't ignore the feelings Rachel stirred in me, and a part of me hoped Joanna wasn't the end of that part of my story. Joanna would have wanted me to find love again, not to be alone, to find someone to grow old with, maybe even have children, too.

"I don't know if I will or not," I replied, tentatively. "You?"

Rachel shrugged. "Perhaps." She looked away for a moment. "You're probably wondering what happened with my marriage."

"Well, I figured I'd learn one day."

"I was in love with him when I was in high school. He was two years older than me. We got married right after graduation. After about three years, he was having 'late nights' at his real estate office, and that turned into him not coming home at all."

"I see."

Rachel nodded and kept her eyes averted from mine. "He'd get really angry. For our fourth wedding anniversary, I made supper for us. And when he was late, I asked where he'd been. He responded by screaming at me, threw a plate, then ran over and punched the cabinets beside my head. A few days later I found a condom in his pocket while washing laundry. That was it."

"I'm sorry to hear that," I offered. It was all I knew to say.

Rachel nodded and kept her face toward the warmth of the last rays of sun. "Before I got married, I'd see women getting divorced early, and I wondered how it ever went wrong for them. They were so in love in the beginning, but within a few years the couples hated each other. I swore that would never happen to me, and then it did."

"Well, I never thought I'd be widowed," I admitted.

Rachel nodded and after some silence, she said something that I sensed she had wanted to say all along. "Thank you for what you did for my family." I turned my face to hers and watched her, waiting for her to finish. "I know my dad hasn't said anything much about it but…"

"No, it's okay," I interrupted. "He didn't have to. I saw it in him, in his voice, too." Rachel looked out across the sea. I sensed relief in her. "How did you guys find the vineyard? How did you hear about it?"

"We came in 1990 or so."

"That was just a few years after I stopped coming," I said.

"Yeah. I was just seven years old. Dad worked on my grandaddy's vineyard in Kentucky. My grandparents migrated over from Hungary. Grandaddy swept floors at a factory while reading books on the English language, and later he applied for a job at a vineyard. Dad met

Mom at a community college, and they got married not long after that."

"Why didn't you go to California?"

"Mom and Dad didn't want to leave the South. Besides, in Napa and Sonoma, it was quadruple the price for land, and the wine market there was saturated. Dad wanted his own vineyard, and he liked Sandra so much that he didn't mind working for someone else. I think he believed he'd buy it from her one day, but that never happened."

"How did he find Grandmother?"

"He called the Chamber of Commerce in Nashville, and they knew Sandra and sent him to her. My parents loved Franklin. It was just a downtown and crossroads back then, as you probably remember. Why did you stop coming down?"

"To Tennessee?" I asked.

"Yeah."

"I think, looking back, lots of things. My parents had died and I didn't want to be pitied. I wanted to be with my friends. I wanted to get a job and make money. Keep my eyes on the girls." I smiled at Rachel after that one, and she let out a small chuckle. "That's how I ended up being a waiter, and then I just gradually fell out of touch with Grandmother. I didn't want to talk about my parents or dwell on what happened. I just wanted to move on and be happy again. I think that's why I came all the way out here."

"To get away from the past."

"Yeah."

"How did your parents pass, if you don't mind me asking?"

"I was seventeen, and they were touring England. Dad rented a car, it was a rainy day, and a truck hit them."

"I'm sorry to hear that."

"Thanks. I was in boarding school in Calgary. In the middle of hockey practice, the headmaster and chaplain came in and asked me to come with them. I'll never forget it. They both had this soft smile, and they were walking slowly, which was unlike both of them. I remember my friends watching me leave, whispering, wondering what kind of trouble I was in. You know, to summon the search party."

I smiled at Rachel, wanting her to understand that I was at peace with that part of my past and could look back on certain facets of it and choose to smile.

"What were they like?"

"My parents?"

"Yeah," she replied.

"They were good people. Dad was generally happy. I remember him finding excitement in stock trading and watching hockey at the pubs with his pals. Mom was a real estate agent, and that kept her busy. She was always trying to be more successful, but I'm not sure anyone has ever figured out what the word 'successful' means.

Grandmother came to the funeral and invited me to move to Tennessee, but I didn't want to, so I went to Pepperdine to start a new chapter. And I did. It was wonderful. But I should've stayed in touch with her. I regret that."

"She loved you," Rachel pointed out. "She missed you a lot."

"I know. I missed her, too."

"She'd talk about you, but she didn't have your phone number."

I felt a tingling sensation and then tears formed in my eyes, but I looked away because I didn't want Rachel to see. I drew a slow breath to help push back the emotion, and when I knew I was level, I spoke again. "I didn't sell the vineyard, because I knew it was the right thing to do. Going back there and seeing it, seeing Finn and Oz there and meeting your family, made me wish I had stayed in touch with her. Those summers growing up were some of the best times of my life."

"So you really did like Tennessee, didn't you? I mean, this past trip."

"Of course I did. Franklin and the vineyard, I loved it. It reminded me of all the good times. It was intoxicating."

Rachel stopped, then I did too. She shifted her weight closer to me, bringing her body within arm's distance of mine. When our eyes met, she smiled. I believed I was beginning to see her true self, and that she was beginning to see mine. Deep down, that's what I had always longed for from anyone, that they know the real me.

The sky was now light streaks of lavender around a fiery fast-sinking sun. The seagulls had left, except for a few that were hurrying toward wiggles in the sand.

Rachel gazed across at the horizon, where the green hills stood as dark silhouettes against the ocean and sky. She leaned into me and I placed my hand on her back, near her shoulders, lightly and carefully. Her cheek grazed my chin while she watched the waves. Her move was bold, but natural. I had forgotten how good it felt to hold a woman I cared for. To breathe in her scent.

"It's so beautiful here," she whispered, breaking the silence. I dropped my hand to the small of her back and felt her body soften. A wind chilled the air and Rachel pulled her arms against her chest and leaned deeper into me.

"I bet with all the books and professors and conversations you have, it's really stimulating here," she said, looking up at me.

"Yeah, but that can get on your nerves after a while, too." Rachel chuckled, and lay her head against my shoulder. "We should probably get back," I suggested, knowing it would be dark soon and that they had a flight to catch. I could have kissed her, and sometimes I wonder what would have happened if I had, but I didn't believe the time was right.

As we walked back toward Oz and Shannon's home, Rachel crossed her arms, shielding herself against the chill. I lifted my hand to rest it on the back of her neck, but stopped myself. I didn't want to rush anything.

"I was wondering," I said. "What was Grandmother like, in her later years?"

"The same," Rachel replied, smiling. "She was a real go-getter. Passionate."

"I wish Finn and Eden could have been here," I surmised. "And I wish they could've met her. You'd like them a lot. I know you met Finn, but you didn't get a chance to really know him, and you would have loved Eden."

"I'm sure I would. Eden's a beautiful name," she replied.

"She's a good one, on the inside and out. Perhaps one day we'll see her."

I didn't mean to use the word "we" but it just came out. I saw Rachel smile, and I wondered what she was thinking. When we made it back to the condo, I caught a glimpse through the sliding glass door of Michael, Oz, and Shannon sitting on the living room sofa. They were flipping through some old photo albums from college and filling Michael in on all the stories. I wished Rachel didn't have to leave, and I guessed that she felt the same.

When I reached for the sliding glass door, I looked back at her, and our eyes locked. I wanted to kiss her, and I knew she wanted it too, but I saw Michael coming to the door.

"We were just about to call you two," he said, when I opened it. "We don't need to miss our flight." They didn't have to be at the airport for another two hours, but I knew Michael didn't want to risk getting stuck in traffic or having rental car problems.

We said our goodbyes and as Michael spoke his parting words to Oz and Shannon, Rachel took a step toward me and we wrapped our arms around each other. Though our hug was short, it was tight and warm, and something we both needed.

When she pulled back, a lock of her hair fell from behind her ear, and into her face. I took it in my fingertips and tucked it back. My hand brushed against her cheek, which was soft as powder, and I felt my heart surge. She looked away and pressed her lips together, and I think she wanted to stay, but we both knew that wasn't realistic. Not yet, anyway.

When she and Michael left, I saw her look back over her shoulder, and I could tell she watched me in the side mirror as they drove away. That old feeling of the beautiful emptiness swept over me, which only those who have loved and lost would understand. And now with Rachel, I would have more beautiful memories of times I knew couldn't last because of the space between us. The bitter sweetness of it all.

"No matter how bad the world gets–" suddenly I heard Grandmother's words, reverberating in the depths of my being. "You'll always have a home here and people who love you." She had spoken those words to me when I was just thirteen years old. She never wanted me to forget them, and I never did. I did have a home in Tennessee, but now, I had to return to my condo, alone again.

Chapter 18

Weeks passed, and I carried on at school as before. Oz said he saw me smiling a bit more, but added that I seemed distracted. I think he thought it was about Joanna or maybe all the papers and class preparation, but my mind kept returning to Tennessee, to that place of safety and comfort.

I never told Oz what was happening inside me. I'm like Finn that way. When something is sacred to us, we hold it within for a long time, until we feel ready to share it with others.

At night, in the solitude of my bedroom, I felt a chill I hadn't noticed before. The coastal wind made that side of the condo cold and my bedsheets icy.

I missed knowing that the Youngs were just across the vineyard. When I sat at my kitchen counter eating supper alone at night, I remembered eating around their dinner table, surrounded by the warmth of family and home-cooked meals and Rachel singing and strumming the guitar.

Family. Was that what I longed for? I had my friends at Pepperdine, but it didn't feel the same. Oz and Shannon, my fellow faculty and students, they would never fully replace what Joanna, my parents, and Grandmother had been to me.

When I walked through the halls of Pepperdine, greeting the students, faculty, and staff, my mind wandered to downtown Franklin. I pictured a warm, sunny Saturday, with men and women dressed in pastels and sunglasses, and balloons tied to the wrists of children. Dogs barked at each other, yapping and licking the ankles of passersby. Bubbles launched from the awning above the candy store and painters sat on stools with easels at street corners. Musicians stood on the sidewalks, or leaned on window sills, playing guitars with their cases open for tips.

The people cruised through, but not too fast, so they could savor the sights and sounds of the town. Old stores had been renovated. Sidewalks were freshly paved, and every ten feet there stood ample green ash trees, their leaves rustling in the breeze. The quaintness of all the cafés, coffee shops, and boutiques, and the general hospitality and kindness of the Tennesseans.

Then I imagined being at Grandmother's, surrounded by the peace and serenity of vineyards, red barns, and green pastures, the deer and rabbits that graze at the trees' edge, the lightning bugs and songs of crickets and frogs.

I didn't try to drive those daydreams away. I knew from experience that feelings aren't to be ignored. We feel for a reason. We should embrace feelings and let them pass in their own time. The important thing, I knew, was not to dwell on thoughts that are bad or negative. I reminded myself that yes, I did miss Tennessee, and its countryside, and Rachel and her family, and that was okay. I could return and visit them anytime I wanted.

I joined other professors for coffee on campus, and sometimes Irish stouts and German ales in the local pubs. When the subject of grief arose, they all said the same thing: the feelings will pass.

I visited Oz and Shannon in their home often, hoping that would lighten things. Oz and Shannon hugged each other and whispered "I love you" when they passed by each other, no matter who was around. Just as Joanna and I had. I always thought it was beautiful to see. But now, watching them left me feeling lonelier.

More weeks passed, and at the end of the summer semester, I stood in my ethics class, speaking to the students about Frankl's *Man's Search for Meaning.* "When we're stripped of everything," I said, paraphrasing him, "only two things will keep us alive and going: having loved ones surrounding us, and knowing we have a mission for our lives. A mission only we can accomplish. That's what gives life meaning. Those two principles are what kept the survivors alive and encouraged in the concentration camps."

As the students wrote their notes, some finishing earlier than others, my mind drifted away to Rachel, her family, and our vineyard.

The semester ended and I entered my grades into the computer. I was sitting in my office chair, staring out the window. Outside, sheets of rain pounded and streamed down the window panes.

I thought about chairing the department the following year, and all the additional responsibilities it would entail. In a few days I would meet with Dean Davis, and he would award me the position. Deep down, I wasn't even sure if I wanted it anymore, so I did all I knew to do. I called Oz and asked if we could go grab a coffee.

"Yes," he said. "But under one condition."

"What's that?"

"Do you have any more Cubans?" Yes, I did. I kept them in the bread box in the kitchen, for special occasions.

We met at the former Diedrich's, now a Starbucks, across from Coogie's. During the day, retired men smoked hand-rolled cigarettes and read newspapers on the terrace. They were all regulars and knew each other by name. The women wore sunglasses and ordered frozen blended drinks like "Skinny Mocha Frappuccino–almond milk–light sugar–no whip."

When I approached the door, I smelled the coffee and the scorched chocolate from the croissants. I saw Oz through the window, already sipping a coffee and reading the newsfeed on his phone. I walked in and ordered a decaf mocha because it paired great with a cigar.

We sat alone outside by the fountain, in a warm

coastal breeze. Oz had brought a lighter, and we lit the cigars. A stone's throw away, pigeons roosted in the rafters and cooed lazily back and forth, as if singing each other to sleep.

When I spent time with Oz, I felt the same comfort I felt with Finn. Finn would always listen first, talk a bit to make sure he understood everything, and then share his thoughts. Oz would listen, too, but his responses came much quicker.

Finn and Oz were special because they had seen me at my highs and lows, they knew all my goods and bads, and they still called me a friend. I hoped they could say that I was that kind of friend to them, too.

The fountain burbled, and we nursed our coffees while propping our feet on opposite chairs and puffing our cigars.

"Are you glad to be back?" Oz asked. I could tell he wasn't making small talk.

"Yeah, but it's different."

"You mean you're different," he argued.

I nodded. "I didn't think I'd ever want to leave Pepperdine, or get tired of it, but ever since I've been back…"

"You've been wishing you were in Tennessee."

"Yeah."

"I understand. If Shannon had asked me to move up north, I would have."

"You want to hear something funny?" I asked him, and I knew he would. "It was something you said at Coogie's: That I was a gentleman. I never really thought of it that way, and would probably have laughed it off if it had come from someone else, but it made me feel good. I'm not used to being single and it's hard making new friends. Everyone has their friends or wives or are set in their ways.

For a while, I thought something was wrong with me. You know, like I was socially awkward and people didn't know how to take me, but looking back, Joanna dying had destroyed me, and I didn't know what normal was anymore."

"There's no such thing as normal," Oz answered.

"I know," I replied. My mind wandered and I remembered once asking Finn and Oz if they thought I was going crazy. They said no, that I was just fine, but I had to ask them to make sure. When your heart's broken, you can't think straight and you second-guess everything.

I had an education, I came from a mentally, emotionally, and economically stable family. I owned the condo I lived in, and I had a great job. Now I even owned a highly appraised vineyard in the old South, but I was single, and so often lonely. How could I have such stability and still be single? People look at you differently when you're not part of a pair. As if everyone should be married, and if not, there's something wrong with you.

What I wanted to tell the world, even though I knew other people's opinions shouldn't matter to me, is this: that I loved a woman with every fiber of my soul and my being, and losing her ripped out my heart. I needed a break for a few years, maybe even for the rest of my life.

"I wouldn't mind moving to Tennessee," I said to Oz, waking from my reflections. "But I've worked so hard to get to where I am."

Oz knocked a thumb of ash off the end of his cigar. "Ryan, if we live to be ninety, our lives aren't even half over yet. I know you and Joanna wanted to have kids, but you can get married and have kids with someone else. Sometimes we have to let go of old dreams in order to embrace new ones."

I don't think Oz understood the depths and wonders of what he had just said, but I knew that statement might just change my life. Oz sat quietly, taking a puff off his cigar and gazing at the fountain. The milky smoke rose in front of his face in the moonlight. The image of him was timeless, and some time between that moment and my drive back to campus that night, I made the decision.

When I entered my condo, I picked up my phone and called Michael.

Chapter 19
1 Week Later

The fall festival had launched at Franklin Vineyard. People were scattered everywhere, eating and drinking at tables, lying on blankets. Long lines curved out the door for wine tastings. Kids chased each other, playing tag and hide-and-seek. The jazz band was in full swing.

Wanda, the office assistant, was pouring the tastings, while Julie was outside refilling water glasses for guests sitting beneath the trellis. Rachel was in the back searching for the last bottle of Cabernet 7, our vineyard's best vintage. It sold for $125. That was back when any bottle from any vineyard that sold for more than $25 was overpriced. But the Youngs couldn't keep this one in stock, so they kept jacking up the price, and it kept selling anyway.

I sat chatting with Wanda and the patrons, learning about their favorite wines. Rachel brought the bottle from the back and found me there standing at the bar. The swinging door lingered open behind her, and just as our eyes met, the door swung back and hit her elbow, and Rachel dropped the bottle. The Cabernet 7 shattered on the floor, and wine splattered everywhere.

Rachel's face turned as red as the Cabernet, and she grabbed a roll of paper towels from the counter, cursing under her breath. She went to her knees, wiping up the mess. I rushed over to help, squatting and gathering the broken pieces.

"I'm sorry. I'm so sorry," she said, over and over.

"It's okay," I answered. Rachel ran to the back sink, dumped the paper towels, and returned with bath towels. I took the glass shards out to the garbage.

I threw the broken pieces away.

"It was our last bottle. Our best."

"It's all right," I whispered. "It's just wine."

"There's a mop and bucket in the side room," offered Wanda, and when Rachel shot a stern look at her, Wanda pressed her lips together and turned back to assist the guests.

Rachel gathered the wine-soaked towels, and jogged to the sink through the swinging door. She was rinsing them out when I came up behind her. The sound of the swinging door and my footsteps were drowned out by the rushing water. When she rung out the towels and turned around, she bumped into me and jumped.

"Stop sneaking up on me!" she snapped, an embarrassed look spreading across her face. She closed her eyes and huffed. "What are you doing here?" she asked, now softer.

Unaffected by her reaction, I didn't say anything, but

I reached for her hand. When we touched, I felt electricity and calmness take over us.

"What are you doing here?" she whispered again, looking up at me. When our eyes met, I saw her face lighten from a dark red to pink. I brushed the hair out of her face. I wasn't sure what to say. What would she think of me moving here? What if our time at the beach was just her heart fluttering, and nothing more?

In my dumbfounded state, I just looked at her. I had rehearsed what I wanted to say in my head, but when I stood in front of her, the words went out the window. "Everyone's missed you," she managed to say, swallowing hard.

"Well, I'm thinking about moving here," I confessed. To my relief, a smile of gladness opened across her face.

"What about California?"

"I thought I'd sell the condo. It'll get me out of debt and even let me live off the profits for a few years. What do you think?" When she nodded, I went on. "What I'm asking, I guess, is if I move here, would you go out on a date with me?"

She smiled even larger, and I knew her answer was yes. "If you're lucky," she replied, clucking her tongue and popping me on the chest.

"I'll need a job," I added. "I'm not an accountant, so I don't want to stare at numbers all day."

Rachel let the towels drop into the sink. "You want to work at Edison's?" she teased.

"Is that where you want to put me?" I replied, playfully.

"Well, what's your experience in the fancy restaurant business?" she asked, like I was being interviewed.

"No more than what you've seen," I answered.

"You have any credentials in the wine industry? We serve it at the vineyard, you know." She tried to stifle a giggle, but it wasn't working.

"No credentials in that," I admitted. All tension between us had drained and talking with Rachel just felt easy.

"So why in world would I hire you? You'd be terrible." Both of our laughs broke free, and I ran my fingers over her hand. When she didn't pull back, I tucked a lock of her hair behind her ear. I felt her shiver with delight.

"Because... I'm a decent guy, I'm intelligent," I went on. She kept looking intently into my eyes, still smiling. "I work hard, and I'd like to be here with you for a while, if that's okay." She leaned back against the counter. I took a quick step and reached around her, placed a hand on the small of her back, and pulled her close.

She drew a shaky breath and wrapped both of her arms around my neck. Her eyes moved to my lips, then back to my eyes again, and when I saw that same unashamed and unabashed desire, I kissed her softly on her lips, and then her neck. My hands slid to her hips, and Rachel gasped and pulled back. "Someone might come in," she whispered. "But later," she added.

Rachel led me outside.

I walked around with her and helped refill all the glasses at people's tables. I helped Michael and Charlie unload a new shipment of wine from a truck. Michael kept rattling off all the tasks that needed to be done after the festival.

During a quick break, I unloaded my suitcase from my rental car and set it in Grandmother's living room. I wondered how my life would change if I ended up resigning from Pepperdine and spending the rest of my life in Tennessee. Finn and Oz would get their wish to have a vineyard to retreat to, and I'd treat them and their wives as honored guests. The idea made me smile.

I thought about all the chapters of my life up to that moment. Life isn't a destination where, at some point, everything will be better, forever. It's not a series of mountains and valleys. It's more like a two-way street where there are beauties and mishaps, conveniences, and inconveniences, constantly coming and going. It's our attitude and our responses that make or break us. Things don't always go as we plan, but that's okay. Sometimes life is just closing some old chapters and opening some new ones.

I will miss Joanna forever. I'll miss the days when Finn and Oz were my roommates back in college, where our greatest concerns were our crushes on girls or the next exam. I'll miss my childhood at the vineyard, and I'll miss my parents, but I'm alive and enjoying life right now, and I believe I'll enjoy it forever, no matter what comes my way.

The sun began to set and I joined Rachel on the front balcony of the shop, which overlooked the grandeur of the rolling hills. Many guests were climbing into their cars and leaving, while others were arriving for the fires and evening jazz. The sky was evolving from a sugary yellow with clouds like cotton balls into shades of violet like the color of ripe grapes. The Tennessee sun was definitely different than the California one, but it would certainly do.

Rachel rested her head on my shoulder, I put an arm around her, and she whispered, "Welcome home. I'm glad you've finally come. The vineyard needed to stay in your family."

Home. Family. I liked the sound of that.

The End

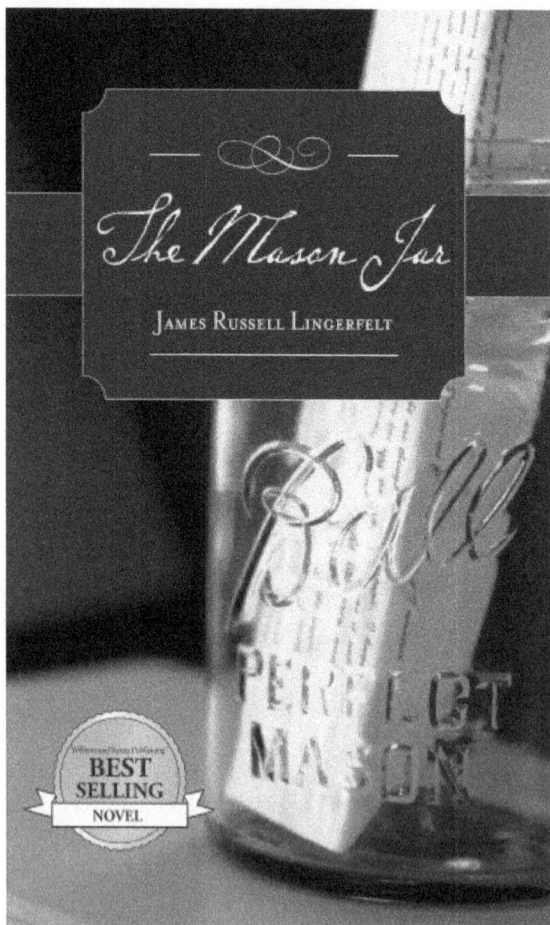

The Mason Jar

What if your old college roommate called, raving about a book someone sent her, calling it the most beautiful book she's ever read? "But," she said, "it's about you." The author is your college ex.

In *The Mason Jar*, Clayton "Finn" Fincannon is a Tennessee farm boy raised at the feet of his grandfather. He and his grandfather leave letters for each other in a Mason jar on his grandfather's desk; letters of counsel and affirmation. When Finn attends college in Southern California, he meets and falls in love with a dark, debutante from Colorado. However, when an unmentioned past resurrects in her life and she leaves, Finn is left with unanswered questions.

Finn goes on to serve as a missionary in Africa, while he and his grandfather continue their tradition of writing letters. When Finn returns home five years later to bury his grandfather, he searches for answers pertaining to the loss of the young woman he once loved. Little does Finn know, the answers await him in the broken Mason jar.

A story about a girl who vanished, a former love who wrote a book about her and a reunion they never imagined.

Written for the bruised and broken, *The Mason Jar* is an inspirational romance that brings hope to people who have experienced disappointment in life due to separation from loved ones.

Alabama Irish

Brian was raised on "the wrong side of the railroad tracks" in inner-city Alabama. Now, at nineteen, with a troubled past and juvenile record, Brian struggles to earn a living and find a life purpose. When he journeys to New York on a chance trip, Brian meets and falls in love with Shannon; a bright eyed, aspiring actress from California.

Brian returns to Alabama stirred by Shannon's courage and passion for life. With a new zest and reason for living, Brian is determined to turn himself into a man worthy of her love. Unable to afford college, Brian discovers the Os Guinness Scholarship, which provides free tuition to Pepperdine University for Irish students who desire to train for Ireland's ministry. With some innovative thinking, Brian fakes his Irish citizenry, accepts the scholarship, and moves to Southern California to attend school and pursue Shannon.

However, when Brian visits Alabama, all the lies come crashing down and Brian comes face to face with a past he thought was finished. Now, Brian must make a choice: lose Shannon by spinning more lies and choosing vengeance in hopes of putting his past to rest. Or choose honesty and forgiveness and embrace a new life with the only woman he ever loved.

Alabama Irish will make us sit back and laugh, then lay the book down and cry. But in the end, we'll reminded that no matter our pasts, the possibility to find true love again is never lost.